Food for L.I.F.E.

Lasting Impressions Forever Enjoyed

Lisa W. Beckwith

KNIGHTDALE, NORTH CAROLINA

Lisa W. Beckwith
www.lisabeckwith.com

Book Cover Design and other services provided by
Rain Publishing.

Food for L.I.F.E./ Lisa W. Beckwith. -- 1st ed.
ISBN: 978-1-7328709-0-1

Library of Congress: 2018961449

Acknowledgements

This book was inspired by my innermost awareness of what life means to me.

The features in this book are strategically based on the human stages of life and supported with scriptures. Sharing this journey with you is an honor, because you did not have to select my book. I hope that you will digest every word and gain from my mastermind focus questions and scriptures.

I hope that you will reflect on the stages closely in each chapter. I pray that you will never give up on you. As long as we have breath in our bodies, we can learn and improve who we are and what our purpose is on earth. I must take this moment to thank my Creator for allowing me this opportunity and season to pour into the lives of His people. I thank Him for showing me who I am and what affects me. I want to thank my precious children for encouraging me daily to never give up on my life, dreams, and them. I am so blessed and fortunate that God blessed me with my four gifts and grandson. Their words have inspired me to be a better mom and when they share how blessed they are to have me as their mom it is indescribable.

Thanks to my big brother and baby sister for loving me, teaching me, and supporting me and my dreams. I love you both dearly. I cannot end my thoughts without giving words of love to my parents. Mom, thank you for your sweet love and support. I admire my mom because she taught me the true meaning of a woman. I am who I am because of her. She taught children for over 30 years and enjoyed every moment. People in our community admire her so much and for that alone I am grateful. My mom has battled with lupus for a very long time and yet she still stands strong, looks beautiful and trusts God every day. If she can stand against adversities, I know I can. Dad, thank you for being a provider for our family. I learned how to work with integrity, structure, and have precise detailed organizational skills because of you.

Thank you to my loving, supportive, and caring family and friends.

My final appreciation goes to my beloved. He has always believed in me. We will forever share four amazing children and an awesome grandson.

I have learned that after every storm I have dealt with in my L.I.F.E. I have always seen a beautiful rainbow that showed me everything would be alright. I hope you relish in Food for L.I.F.E. (Lasting Impressions Forever Enjoyed).

Kindly,

Lisa W. Beckwith

CONTENTS

INTRODUCTION

I wrote this book for individuals to identify each stage of human development and how negative events during childhood and adolescence can influence later phases of life if early wounds are not healed. I related the phases of life to the courses of a meal to illustrate what is necessary for growth at each stage through a seven-step awareness process. If we get the right portions at each phase, we can enjoy life and properly handle the emotions of being overwhelmed, frustrated, and discouraged.

The Mastermind questions included after every chapter are to help you reflect on what you read and consider how to apply it to your life. Once you have made that connection, you can complete the Finish-These-Sentences exercises to help you to stay true to YOU and your commitment. The A-Z Scriptures can help you balance out your thought process and reflect on the promises of God to you. God did not create us to be perfect; instead, He gave us instructions on how to live right by following His Word. God's principles can guide you to have a life that reflects Lasting Impressions Forever Enjoyed! This book will help you to walk away from a complete course in life feeling and looking satisfied! "Life is to serve and be served!" -LWB Butterfly

CHAPTER ONE

THE APPETIZER

Childhood

"How to overcome any childhood pain"

This dish is a mini served portion right before the meal is received. It is the stimulator for the other course to come. The developmental stage for people works just the same. We all start out very small and then our course of life increases. I do not have many memories of my early childhood, but the parts I do remember are good moments and feelings. My mother and father lived in North Carolina most of their lives, but as time went on, they wanted to start a new journey in a new area. My dad moved the family to Washington, D.C. in 1970. That is where

I was born, but it was short-lived. By the time I was two, they decided to move back to North Carolina because of a home invasion. My mama told daddy that she did not want to live there anymore; it wasn't where she wanted to raise her family.

Mama always enjoyed sharing things with me about events in my life. She loved to tell me about the time she took pictures of me wearing a yellow ruffle dress with my hair in curls. She was very disappointed that I never had a chance to see the photos; most of my baby pictures were taken during the robbery. I do not have any memories of my time in D.C. because I was very small. Mama told me I was a peaceful, quiet, loving, and happy child. She once told me the story of how I gained my nickname from one of mama's in-laws. One day, when I was at the table, I put my hand in a bowl of mashed potatoes, and from that point on I was called "Tata". I loved hearing stories like that from mama. She helped me to see what kind of person I was from the beginning and that I am still that same person to this day. My identity was present at birth.

Most of us do not remember how we were as babies, and we must rely on others' views of our actions until we start to see them for ourselves. If we think about the life span of an infant, for example, we see, within the first 18 months what a child is lacking regarding the ability to speak and use language skills to articulate all their feelings about what they know, what they want, and what their needs are. Without being able to verbalize what they need, a child depends on their caregivers and learns to trust.

Think about it for a moment. The most important part of human development starts with a person not being able to say anything regarding their feelings. They cannot express their thoughts and cannot protect themselves. Babies cannot speak but they will scream, react uncomfortably, and refuse to go to a person voluntarily. It's the parent's job to determine what is wrong with their child and address the issues or remove the child from danger. God is the same way. As adults we can articulate how we feel when we are being mistreated. God is there to help us work through our feelings of discomfort when we feel threatened by a person's treatment of us. He gives us signs well before major issues develop. Sometimes we ignore the signs because we are more focused on what we think we need. Let's ponder. Your inner man knows something is not right in a situation, even if you don't fully understand it.

When that happens to a baby, they automatically respond with a "cry out" or some form of sound indicating their discomfort. Now, as an adult, you must respond differently by speaking up for yourself and saying, "You are mistreating me and I refuse to continue to involve myself with your behavior any longer. It is time for me to separate myself from you and position myself in a better environment and situation." I am not saying for you to remove yourself every time someone is being harsh or aggressive with you, simply be wise enough not to put yourself back in that situation again. Just as Maya Angelou said, "Do your best until you know better. When you know better you will do better." Mistreatment leads to mistrust. The wounded child within may want to cry, scream, and have a tantrum, however, as an adult it is time to handle mistrust in more of a mature way. By operating in wisdom and identifying your insecurities you will respond better when it comes to expressing your emotions.

Although a child does not use words to express their feelings, they can communicate what does not feel right. If our instincts start at the preliminary stage, we must connect that with our adult stage as well. Knowing how we should be treated starts at birth. Trust develops when parents or caregivers show how much they really care and do not display reckless behavior. Mistrust is also learned during the early stages of life when those who are supposed to care for the child repeatedly neglect or harm them.

The way infants learn to respond to people is built on whether they can or cannot trust the person who is taking care of them. It is amazing how strong our senses are as humans that we can pick up good and bad energy at that age. Theologian Eric Erikson calls this phase the "oral sensory stage". This stage is focused on how the mother responds to her child, for example: does she respond positively, or does she give her child negative energy? When a child experiences a loving response, that is when they begin to trust and feel secure. This skill is something that we continue to build on throughout life. In general, we tend to respond to people the way they respond to us, the golden rule. It is also a defense mechanism.

Trust is a feeling and to get it, you should be a person who gives it. We must feel comfortable and trust if we are going to spend time with someone or build a future. If trust is broken, one may become exasperated due to unfulfilled desires. If these wounds are not healed, we can begin to shut down and not want to trust anyone. Once this happens, it can be very hard for the next person to gain our trust, so we must start identifying the triggers as to why we may not trust. If you really want to understand yourself, find out where your lack of trust began that caused your "love connection" not to be activated. Was it during the stage when you were supposed to have been nurtured by parents, or did it happen later in your life when you were disappointed by others? If you did not receive the proper care early, you may be oblivious to what trust and love look like. It is very important for people to receive love and care as early as possible to avoid the feeling of isolation.

We are designed to give and receive affection in a loving, caring, pure, and Godly way. If we do not experience this, we become withdrawn and then respond in rebellion without understanding why. We must strive to be loving adults and then our children will inherit that gift. If not, we will continue to create a cycle of hurt from generation to generation. We must realize that healthy cycles begin with the first contact a child has with their mother, father, family members, or caregivers.

Having identified the problem, be assured that you can grow in love and trust. This knowledge can transform negative behaviors in our society if we use it to obtain healing and have healthy relationships. We must make this change, so that the next generation can have a better opportunity to trust than we possibly did. As we get older, we must remember God is here to keep us safe because He is our parent. When we make bad choices, He deals with us just like we do when we must correct children. We must all work together to make sure no child feels unsafe and like they cannot trust because of how someone treated them. Our Creator does the same thing with us. The bible is our guide and we should trust His words will protect us. We know that as babies we needed help with everything the first few years of our lives. If we did not get the nurturing that we needed, we would struggle in our development. We are really created to interact with others. Now is the time for us to make sure we are learning the right way to treat one another.

In the beginning, God created Adam and knew that Adam needed someone to support him, so God gave him someone he could trust and share his life with. Having someone you trust is important, however not everyone can be trusted, so just be mindful and use wisdom when allowing someone to come into your space. We do need to safeguard ourselves and know that God's desire is to safeguard us from the enemy. Those who raised us may not have understood how to protect us, but as we grow in understanding we must rely on God for our protection. It is our choice to surrender and become vulnerable enough to trust. If trust is hard for you to do, let go of fear. It is time for you to stand up and say, "I will not allow myself to be fooled by my own insecurities anymore. I must become better at sharing and being willing to be transparent with others."

Everyone is not out to get you. Trust may be a challenge for you, but now is the time to soul-search, dig deep into your hurts, and lift the dirt that has hardened your heart. It is time to admit how you feel about trusting and understand why you feel that way.

The next phase of a child's life is between 18 months and three years of age, the "toddler" stage. During this stage, a child develops basic strength and awareness of their self-sufficiency and limitations. We can relate this to all the core situations that we deal with in life. Self-esteem is how a person views themselves. Mama and Daddy did a pretty good job of making sure I felt good about myself. Mama would make sure I did not look inappropriate when we were in public and daddy made sure that I did not feel bad about my size. I was a very heavy little girl growing up and if my parents had made me feel bad about myself, I think my self-esteem would have been low. I already felt different and if I had to hear bad things coming from my parents, it really would have made me feel even worse. Mama had a way of encouraging me with her words. She caused me to think about my image of beauty instead of pressuring me about it. As I got older I saw that my parents' love toward me was no different than God's. He tells us what we need to work on to be a better person for ourselves and does it in a loving way. For those who did not have this type of treatment with their earthly parents, I pray that you now can surrender and start having this with your Creator (if you have not done so already).

If no one has told you that they love you, please let me take this time to say, "I LOVE YOU" and I mean it from the bottom of my heart. I may not personally know you, but one thing is true, I know that love conquers all, and, most importantly, you matter. I know that for you to love yourself, you must first believe in yourself as God does. I know that being hurt and not trusting could block you from seeing your worth, when you allow negative relationships to identify you. Today, you can start identifying yourself as being a loving and caring person who is full of purpose. It is time to cherish yourself. Authenticity is a unique quality! Do not ever be ashamed of Your Own Uniqueness (YOU). When people become confident in who they are, the way others treat them won't negatively impact their self-esteem. When you know that you are uniquely made, how someone else views you will not matter at all. You will understand that they have the right to their opinion of you. I know that is easier said than done, but most of us really depend on what others think of us more than on what we think of ourselves. When we truly know who we are, then what others think just won't matter. If you are a people-pleaser, STOP, because you can never measure up to most people's standards. It is okay to hear someone's opinion but remember not to abandon God's principles and morals for the sake of COMPROMISING good character traits. We often try to work on ourselves from the outside. It really should be revised. People need to see one another from the inside out. If we spend time fixing up our inner man as much as we try to fix up the outer man, we may not struggle with low self-esteem as much.

It may seem hard to value yourself if you have lacked love and support in your life. It is time to begin building a stronger view of who you are and respect yourself even if others do not. You do not have to wait to be validated, you can validate yourself. If others have issues with who you are and what you do, that is their problem, not yours. The more confident you are, the more you will love who you are. Be a person who shows the world that you have self-love and be determined to live a good life without being egotistical. God wants us to be strong and of good courage, but if we do not have a balance, we can reflect negative vibes. He does not want us to be disruptive and critical toward ourselves nor others. I have learned, to have self-esteem I must find peace. The happiest place you can escape to is having an inner peace with who you are. It is time for a vacation! LWB Butterfly. It does not mean that you must physically take a trip. Just keep freeing your mind and know that you deserve the right to love yourself in a healthy way.

In the process of loving yourself, you must learn to speak the truth about who you are, what you have experienced, and what you want. Sometimes people think that not saying something is okay, but really silence can be harmful. If you do not share how you feel, you will allow a negative build-up to form inside of you. Do not be your own prisoner. We cannot trap ourselves in and then one day explode because we never learned how to speak up for ourselves. That reaction is just an adult tantrum. We know that most children have tantrums when they are disciplined. For example, imagine being in a store and your child wants something that you did not go into the store for and you tell them that they cannot have it. The child continues to make a scene and the next action is for the parent to react by yelling, spanking, or simply leaving the store. That is the same for us as adults if we have a so-called "tantrum". We will not be physically disciplined by our parents, but we do find that our spiritual Father (God) will show us our wrong behavior and He will teach us a lesson through the Holy Spirit on patience and self-control.

We sometimes fail to realize that self-control is a "Fruit of The Spirit" (Galatians 5:22-23). We must seek God if we desire to really have it. Just as toddlers need courage to transition from crawling to walking, we need to have courage as well to elevate from natural reactions to spiritual reactions. What has always helped me? The serenity prayer. I say it very often, especially when I feel overwhelmed with a situation that I cannot fix. It states "God, grant me the SERENITY to accept the things that I cannot change, the COURAGE to change the things I can and the wisdom to KNOW the difference." What I discovered from this is that God wanted me to understand that I must not put my energy and focus into fixing anyone but myself. The courage is for changing me and not anyone else. I have learned that if I do not care or like something that is happening outside of me, then I must simply go into prayer. The main thing I had to understand is I am the one with the problem; therefore, I am the one who needs redirection. People will do what is pleasurable to them and I have nothing to do with it even if it affects me. As I speak on this I must include the fact that God has given us all free will. It is up to us to want to make right or wrong choices.

Let's think about toddlers. They must master basic skills for themselves. They learn how to walk, talk, and feed themselves and that is what helps them become less dependent on their guardian(s). Independence requires them to develop their motor skills, toilet training, and many other skills needed to grow up. The purpose is for the child to learn how to control their own bodies so they do not have accidents and learn how to hold their own spoons so they can feed themselves. We often think when a child says "no", their response is disrespectful, but if we are impartial to the situation, they are showing signs of their God-given will (just like adults). We will tell people no when we do not want to do something. If we do not learn how to say no to things we will become exposed. It is time to walk in a better awareness of the word. If "NO" feels harsh, you are simply "Needing Opportunity" in that instance. Turn that barrier into a "New Opportunity" LWB Butterfly.

Remember to love God and then yourself and everything else falls in line. Lucille Ball once said, "You really have to love yourself to get anything done in this world." This mentality helps so much. We must understand that saying no for whatever reason, is ok, however we must in turn be able to accept the word no as well. While toddlers learn to say "no" they also need to learn how to accept "no". Learning this early will help an individual not to believe they can get everything that they want. If you struggle with the word "no" think on how you handled it when you were younger. I remember telling my children that "no" is an answer that you may not like, however, it is important to understand that "you get what you get and do not have a fit". This is what psychologists call emotional regulation. Disintegrations are going to happen. However, it is important to know this is a process and if taught correctly, a person will respond correctly.

The next stage of childhood is the "school age" that starts from six to 12 years old. This season causes a child to have opinions about their environment in complex ways as they develop abstract thinking and clear communicative skills. The youngsters frequently change from being simple thinkers to developing a strong inner conscience. Their reasoning is sensible concerning social events. Their minds become more intellectual and able to answer challenging questions with ease. The communication becomes more mature than before. Before this point a child would not be concerned about doing things the right way or not, but now they are making sense of things and understanding that mistakes are a part of life. Our parents knew we were going to make mistakes and they were there to help us. If you were a child who did not receive guidance, your choices during this time were probably not beneficial. If you did not receive any correction during this time, it may be hard for you to listen to people when they correct you. Children must have boundaries, and if they do not learn this, it is very likely they will continue to function with the mindset that, "I can do what I want and not care what the consequences are." Sometimes, the person you messed up with may not have a calm reaction, but it is important to respond with a gentle tone and not be quick to react aggressively.

When I was this age, my parents were in tune to my personality and responded to me in a way that I would receive, no matter what my actions were. I am a very sensitive person and they knew that about me. Note: Sensitivity is not weakness. I do not like when someone talks harshly to me or tries to purposefully hurt my feelings. It is important for people to understand they can help someone without making the person feel judged. People need to feel loved and cared for, no matter what stage or age in life. I know that during this stage, children may go through so many different mental, physical, and emotional trials. A person's reactions may come from one of these areas and sometimes children do not know how to fully express things that happen to them if they've been placed in a poor situation. It is time to evaluate why you still may be dealing with struggles. You can move on from toxic situations. You can learn how to walk in wisdom and be free. It is time to release the low points and start building up in a new direction by saying, "I know I am human and I know I will make mistakes and mistakes will be made toward me." Balance those two differences and be aware of how to keep your past from negatively affecting your future. If you are not this person, that is okay too. Just remember that you may be a sound-board for someone who is.

I have found that my most challenging stage of life was my adolescent years. How many of you remember this part of your life? For the most part, I think most of us do because we are fully cognitive. We can channel, direct, and identify the relationships we had and how we felt and reacted to them. During this time, we think we are grown but really cannot take care of ourselves. We feel grown, act grown, talk grown, and yet we are so far from it. We think we can tell others what to do, but still need to depend on them. Now, that is funny! Teens often behave as though a parent should only do what they want and not offer any feedback or consequences for unacceptable behavior. During this phase the adolescent experiences increased self-consciousness and may also experience identity issues along with new freedoms and responsibilities.

I remember this age very well. I was 13 and was considered an overweight child. My body was truly out of whack. I used food as my way of escape. My parents did not limit my food intake. Mama explained that when she was growing up, she did not have much. She said that she would never limit her children regarding food because of her experience. Daddy just gave in because I would ask. So, there I was, an overweight child full of love from my parents, and full of their insecurity, which did not help me at all. I needed balance and neither one of them could give it because of their personal issues. So, I ate whatever I wanted with no boundaries. How many of you know that I did have boundaries, but I did not know how to implement them? One summer, a new water park was opening, and my parents told my siblings and I we were going. Well, I never liked going to swim because that meant I had to put on a bathing suit and I did not want to do that. So, I told my dad that I did not want to go. Instead of swimming I went to four chain restaurants and I got a super-sized meal at each one of them in the same day. You may think, how could a parent do that to a child who is already overweight?

I finally grew tired of looking the way I did, so I began to take my weight very seriously and I did something about it. I was tired of hiding behind t-shirts when I went to the pool. I had a childhood best friend (to this very day we are friends) and we made a pact that we would never take off our shirts. I was so determined that I was not going to continue to be the "fat" kid. My brother had always been my best friend and protector. One day, we were at school and I was walking past him and his friends. Suddenly, I heard someone say, "Isn't that CW's little sister?" and then another voice said, "Don't you mean, his big sister?" I was traumatized by that statement. I went home and looked in the mirror and vowed I would never be picked on again because of my weight. I was upset that my parents let me eat so much, but I knew that my parents thought they were helping me. I decided to lose weight on my own. Middle school was big-time, and I was headed there. I just did not want to be big anymore. I knew I had to do something; I just did not know what, exactly. It was all in me, and up to me, to figure out. You know what that did for me, it caused me to "feel grown". I had to make decisions for myself without the support of my parents. I went on a diet. I knew that sweets were not good for me and I loved bread. So, I said, "Lisa, you are going to have to stop eating that stuff and you are going to have to exercise," and I did just that. I entered sixth grade weighing over 150 pounds. Daddy used to drive me to school. To get more exercise, I asked him if I could walk to school. I stopped eating the school meals and brought a small lunch instead. I had a plan and I was not going to rest until that plan was complete. I did this for over a year. By the time school started the next year, I lost the weight. For the first time, people stopped and talked with me, and they could not believe it. They did not know it was Lisa Wesley. They were amazed by how I looked. I went from a size 18 to a 6. I lost over 75 pounds. I was shocked at how people were responding to me because I never received any attention like that before. I even had boys looking at me. Now, you know that was a big deal. My next middle school year was a shocker for everyone. I walked in the gym and people were like "who is that"? No one knew who I was at first. It was a wonderful feeling to be visible, because I had always felt invisible. As I reflect on my moments in middle school, I realized just how independent I really was and how I made such a drastic move for myself at such a young age. At that time, I did not care what my parents thought about my decision to lose weight. I just knew I had to please myself and feel good about me. Once my mind was made up, I changed my physical image.

This showed that I had courage and discipline because I had a goal to reach. During adolescent years, parents are not as influential as peers. If it was up to my parents, I would have stayed the size and weight I was. Within this age bracket, children can and will make decisions that work for their best interest, as I did, but need to remember to have respect for adults who would like to share advice about things. On the other hand, adolescence can appear to have unreceptive and destructive behavior. For instance, I made the weight loss decisions and did not think of anyone else. I believed my situation did not affect anyone else, so I did not wait around for anyone to tell me "I will help you later". I know my brother's friends may not have even meant anything with their words, but I felt self-conscious and that was enough to motivate me to make a change for myself. I remember having very low self-esteem.

A great friend from childhood and I used to do everything together. We first became friends when we were in the 2nd grade. When it was time for us to go back to school in the fall we were going to the 3rd grade and I could not understand why we could not attend the same classes anymore. As I got older I found out why. During that time, students were placed in certain classes based on standardized tests. Well, I found out that I did not score high enough on the standard test, which caused me not to be in the same class as my best friend. I was crushed and dealt with a lot of self-doubt for this reason. I did not understand why I was being analyzed by data and not valued as a person. It is easy to get caught up in "woe is me" and think that you do not have the same opportunities as others. I learned that is why my mindset was not strong enough to fight through hurtful things that affected me. I had to lift myself up with a comeback. Just like my weight loss journey, I had to make a change for myself that I never knew was possible. I had to learn how to deprogram and then reprogram my mindset to fit what I needed. Later in life, I understood that my Creator knew my heart's desire and He helped me to be strong enough to lose weight and start to feel good about myself. God wants us to know that He supports what is in us once we discover it. God is not aggressive with us and sometimes that can be a problem, because we are looking for Him to do all the physical work. Instead, He is teaching us to dig deep, confront our inner man, make connections to what we have within and pull it out. Doing this will cause us to achieve our own personal goals and build ourselves up instead of tearing ourselves down.

We must learn how to reach out to others when we go through things, because we find out that we are not alone. I eventually understood that the school system had an operation that tracked students' growth, which was the reason for my departure from my friend. I had low self-esteem about school for a very long time, because no one took the time to explain the process to me. I know as a child, your parents are supposed to give you everything, but what happens when they do not even know what you need? We must learn how to go to our Creator for guidance. He has given us the power to execute the vision and be confident in it. Remember to build yourself up when you do not like something about yourself. You may be tempted to be harsh on yourself when you learn that you have been doing things incorrectly. You are simply growing and adapting to newness. Thank your Creator for what He is showing you. Thank Him for giving you hope to do what your natural desires are trying to manifest in your life.

The next phase of adolescence is the teenage years. This time can be fun, exciting, confusing, and fearful all at the same time. For me, it was all the above. As a teen, my physical body was so much more mature than I was, which caused me to receive more attention, not just from boys my age but even men. I had to have a strong mind and not become vulnerable to the words and compliments I received.

At one point, I developed an eating disorder, not even realizing it. I did not love myself or like the way I looked. So, I thought not eating would help me get to my weight loss goal. I eventually realized that I was only hurting myself in another way. If I would have shared my feelings with someone (my parents), I may not have gone through that alone. It is just like having a relationship with God. If we are trying to deal with something without His guidance and wisdom, we can put ourselves in a worse position for no reason.

Now I understand that people have their reasons for not sharing difficult things with others, but your lack is possibly someone else's strength. I realized that each one can reach one. Needing someone is not a bad thing. One of my quotes that I love is, "A need for something is not a vulnerable act, instead it is a way to share" LWB Butterfly. For me I did not share at first because I was already hurting, so my thoughts were, "Why share with the people who already did me wrong?" As I matured, I realized that I may not have shared with my parents, but I could have shared with someone else. Maybe you are that person as well. Just pray and see how your Creator will peel away the pain. By nature, I am very shy/quiet and do not speak up for myself, but I had to learn how to voice my opinions and feelings. It was hard for me to do that. Then as I got closer to God, He taught me in His word that "even as a child, we are known by what we do" (Proverbs 20:11). What that taught me was God pays attention to how we feel and act even when we are children. However, in my time, children were seen and not heard. As a child/teen being raised with this mindset, I felt sheltered and alone. I did not know how to break free from this way of thinking. I was living in the box people put me in for a long time.

That is why I am the type of parent I am. I love to hear what is going on in my children's heads, so I can know what is going on in their world. I am grateful that my children love to share deep, hurtful, disappointing things with me, because they know what I am going to do. They know I am there for them as a mother and that when I am alone I will go into my "war room" (Chris Fabry) and pray them through their thoughts, actions, and situations. I know that shame develops in children when they are embarrassed about their feelings and actions. I have learned from my own situations not to make my children feel like I am judging them. I am there for them and they must know it. I did not know my parents really cared because they did not make me feel that way emotionally. I did not want to be a parent who waited to have a relationship with my children when they were older, because most of the time, the damage is done by then.

One thing that is shameful to me is how adults talk so negatively about the younger generations. My question is, "What are we as adults showing them? In our society, everything on TV is produced by an adult, every bad habit is modeled by an adult and yet the adults want children to "do right and make right choices". That, to me, is a double-standard. How can children/teens do right if all they see is the wrong, immoral behavior of adults? Let's stop being hypocrites in the sight of our children. Why? Children need to see great examples. We are not living for their approval; however, we should not blame them if they choose to do wrong because that is the example we show them. Parents should hold themselves accountable. Reflecting on my youth, I realize that growing up prepares you to have an independent life, which is important.

I learned to define myself in High school. When I should have been preparing for an adventure in college, I was planning for parenthood. For me, high school was not a bad experience, because I was surrounded by good friends, but the academic piece was a blur. I was labeled in school, and when that happens a student pretty much skates through their years because of lack of knowledge regarding their situation. At that time, it was being placed in remedial classes. I had to figure it out on my own. I know that is why I longed to be an educator in the first place. I did not want any child to go through the emotional embarrassments of hiding or waiting to go to a classroom because of the type of environment they were in.

During my early time in high school my focus was not on academics. Instead, I spent my time with someone who was very popular and athletic. At first, I did not know what came with being with someone of that caliber. Eventually I did. I found out that being with an athlete means dealing with all the others who want him as well, and he entertained the attention. I could not understand why he would make the type of choices that he made, later causing problems in our relationship. By the time I was ready to move forward without him, I found myself falling in love with him. I also found myself being a mother at eighteen years old, by a person who I ended up marrying and sharing four wonderful children with.

My story was nowhere near a fantasy, but it was one that was spirit-led. When most teenagers are living it up by hanging out and partying, my journey with that was short-lived. I did not want anyone else to raise my son, but I did not know how to raise him myself. At the age of 19 years old, I committed my life to God and I never looked backed on that type of lifestyle again. Now, I was faced with two major responsibilities. One was raising a child, and the other was learning how to live a Christian lifestyle. Both were very challenging, because I did not know what that life looked like. I had to experience the trials as they came. In that process, I could not identify my true self or my talents and abilities. I was focused on helping my son and his father. I truly did not know who I was and what I really wanted. I was a very quiet person, and it was important for me to please others. I believe that it is okay to help others, but it is also necessary to make sure your needs are taken care of as well. I do love seeing people happy and doing what they love. You may be that type of person as well and that is okay. Just remember to be true to yourself in the meantime. Being this type of person can cause a person to possibly take advantage of you. Part of me feels like I was taken for granted.

I am not trying to paint a picture of a victim, but that is exactly what I felt was happening. I did not fully understand that I could make decisions, because what I experienced as a child caused me to feel like I had no choice in any matter. For some reason, people overlooked what I wanted and did what was pleasing to them. Everyone should do what they want, but not at the expense of someone else. One decision that I do not regret is making the decision to have my son. I did not care what anyone (including my parents) felt about it. My son was, and is, my guardian angel. Some people may feel that having a child would have taken from them. It truly gave me life and was such a blessing for me. For the first time, I felt valued. I finally understood what love was and how to give and receive it. My oldest son was/is the best gift in the world because he showed me that something good can come from me. My decision to become a Christian so early was because I was grateful to a God who trusted me to be a mother and knew I would be a responsible one, even with the choice of having him before marriage. I did not know the importance of that either. When I discovered that I should have been married first, I made the decision to commit to God and wait until I was married before having other children.

During my spiritual journey, I had the best pastor in the world who helped me understand that God had great plans for my life and He would help me as a young mother. My pastor was a man of God and I miss him deeply. He passed away December 4, 2015. This man taught me how to depend on God and put my trust in Him, and not man. I am who I am today because of the commitment, love, and dedication I saw my pastor have for Christ. I felt that being a teenage mother was "senseless" and abnormal. I learned that I could raise my son well with God's protection and guidance. It was important for me not to depend on my mother to raise my son. It was up to me. Mama was truly there for me. She never put me down or judged me. She even gave me a baby shower. Back then, that was not something that a mother would do for her teenage child, but she did, and I love her even more for it. She taught me that regardless of what your child may decide, it is important to be there to guide them in a better direction. I felt the most connected with mama at this point in my life. Mama, to this day, is still the same. She loves my children to her core and they love her just as much. All of them have a wonderful relationship with her and it is because of who she is as a person. I Love you Mama!

As a teenager, my son was the best life lesson learned. I do not have any regrets for having him when I did because he saved my life. If I did not have him, I might not have connected with God. As I think about this it really gives me chills, because my life changed for the better. I know being a young parent was not easy, but it was worth it. I have learned so much and I am not ashamed of my story. However, I did choose an accelerated road to adulthood. As a teenager and young adult, I was not able to attend college or any job training opportunities. I was at an age where I still very much depended on my parents while at the same time, having a child to depend on me. Choices like these can bring life-changing experiences. The word choice is very powerful to me and I created a reminder quote. When we make choices, it can create a process that we may not be aware of, but here is something to consider as you are making yours: "C-Clear thoughts, H-Hear from God, O-Obey God's word and will, I- Invest in trust, C-Communicate Honestly, E-evaluate my motives, S-Surrender to my Choices!" LWB Butterfly.

The stages of life are developmental processes. If one area has been damaged, it is a possibility that you may carry negative choices into your current situations. Evaluate your transition from childhood and school-age experiences and see if it was a difficult process. Finding the root of your feelings can help you understand why you respond the way you do. Do not waddle in past decisions if you were not satisfied with them. The time is now for you to sit down and embrace the changes that are happening in your life and come up with a new plan. You may discover that you have a dream that was never nurtured or noticed. Now that you are seeing clearly, you can walk in it and make it happen for yourself.

Forgiving Our Parents

If you did not have a family that spent time together, now you can be the person who does it. Whatever was lacking for you during childhood, you can change, and make it work for you and your current situation. I know, for me, it has always been important to spend time with my children and to really listen to their needs and desires. Spending quality time with my family caused us to put everything aside and focus on individual needs. In my marriage, my husband did not understand me, or even try to understand me when I told him that family trips and quality time were important to me. He said we would do it, but it never happened. I grew up seeing my parents try to make the best of what we had. I remember trips to the lake, beach, and movies. Those were some of my best times. We did not always take grand expeditions. We did, however, spend meaningful time. Only after my marital separation did my children and I experience family vacations. One year, I could not go too far because I lacked financially. I took my baby to the next town and told him we were out of town on a trip and he did not even know the difference. He had the best time, because it was not about where we were. It was a new environment. My effort was good enough. My children were appreciative in this respect. It hurt me that their dad did not value that part of their life as a vital element, because they truly deserved to have memories with him too. I still recollect fond memories of my parents. Those adventures were fun and memorable. To pay it forward and share such times with my children? Priceless. I wanted them to be exposed to a lot of things and cause them to want to venture out on their own one day without being afraid of what the world offers. I also wanted them to experience the world in a positive light. This way, they would know its beauty and vastness.

I think experience alone is a life lesson all by itself. It causes us to be more knowledgeable about the world and to be able to make informed decisions that reflect our interests. Now, if you do this, that is great. If not, that is fine too, but these moments will be a reflection for you and yours in quiet moments. We must learn to navigate life as individuals, not being controlled by our child-like perspectives, especially if they are harmful. I know, as a child, and teen, we all have different experiences. Today is our day of letting go and moving forward as a whole person, one who is not broken into small, unanswered pieces.

It's so easy for us to judge our parents. We tend to forget the good things that they did/do, and our treatment can be harsh when we feel neglected in any way. I know that when we think about things our parents have done, we feel like they owe us something. The truth is, all they did was gave us life. Once we grow up, we should replace our learned behavior with our more developed conscience as adults. Let's ponder. Why do we have that expectation from our parents? If you have children, do you expect them to excuse your mistakes? When we are children, we do not understand that our parents are doing what they think is best for us. I know adults who, to this very day cannot get past the hurt that they experienced as a child and they blame their parents for it.

As much as my children love me, I have gone through turbulence with them as well. My first-born felt that I should have done more for myself and stood up to his dad more than I did. Truth be told, he probably was correct, but I had to figure that out for myself. I still had to teach him to stay in his lane and be my child, not someone who dictated my life. I told him that I was sorry for anything that affected him, including our (his parent's) relationship. However, he was old enough to make choices: choices to forgive and release the hurt and judgmental outlook on myself, choices that would better suit his needs.

I did not want him to have to go to God like I had to and ask Him to show me how to walk in forgiveness. I didn't want him to constantly relive painful memories of what he could not control as a child like I did. I realized that the little girl in me must be healed so that I could be the woman of God that I am now. For a while, I felt mama wanted more from me as an adult than she gave me as a child, and I resented her for that. My internal feelings? "Why does she want me to give her everything now that I am grown, and she did not do the same for me?" Well, I learned that my feelings were real and okay to have. What did it truly do for me though, other than to create negative energy when she needed me? Once I forgave my parents, I started to build a stronger relationship with them and we now have a healthier relationship. God showed me the importance of serving and supporting them. I had to deal with my true feelings about mama. I learned to appreciate her, forgive her, and enjoy the journey with her. I love my mom naturally and spiritually. I understand now that I was engulfed in so much of the past that I was losing time with my true friend (mama). Whether our parents were great or a great disappointment, they gave us the greatest gift a person can give: LIFE. Our parents may not have had the characteristics or abilities to give us what we wanted from them, but I am sure you have come across someone who is able to help you out in your time of need. We all experience disappointment from our childhood, but it is time to walk in what we know is better for us. As Ms. Angelou states, "Know Better, Do Better."

If you are struggling as an adult because of your past, you must decide if you want to keep allowing it to be a road-block. One that keeps you from growing and moving forward in peace. A lot of times, our emotions are like roller coasters, they go up and down. Take a moment and think about your low points, for example: identity issues, conflict with parents, desiring an intimate relationship, prioritizing friends-over-family, and dealing with unhappiness or hopelessness. All these scenarios can result in a disconnection from God, poor grades in school, alcohol or drug use, unsafe sex, etc. These choices exemplify a lack of desire to take care of yourself. You should not be about that life. Identify and break deep-rooted, controlling actions and emotions. As your relationship with God becomes stronger, He will help you cope with it, only if you allow Him to. He teaches us how to have good character traits that will help our behavior. God knows our thoughts. He can lead us to the right people to get the help we need. God is our support, and we should not walk in the flesh, but rather in the spirit that He gave to each of us (2 Corinthians 5:7). That is why we must be able to understand and seek His voice.

The bottom line: God cares for us. We must STOP being our own enemy. God has a way to make you feel joy, love, and peace in an indescribable way. We know that life is full of problems, and the best advice I can give is to allow God to be the solution. As you reflect on your childhood, please remember this, "Remember always that you not only have the right to be an individual, you have an obligation to be one" (Eleanor Roosevelt). "There is something of yourself that you leave at every meeting with another person" (Fred Rogers), and "Low self-esteem is like driving through life with your hand-brake on" (Maxwell Maltz). It's time to walk in newness with yourself, your parents, and anyone who may have hurt you. It is time for you to put childish thinking away and walk in the shoes of adulthood (1 Corinthians 13:11). I realize that maturity is the key to remove a lot of unwanted behaviors and emotions. Heal yourself.

Do not allow your age or situation to stop you from being the mature adult that you are. In life, we have a "normal path" to complete, which begins during school age. After graduation from school, it is up to you to dig deep and figure out what direction you want to go in for your educational and professional advancement. Once you have made your decision, it will be your way of contributing greatness to our society.

MASTERMIND

1.   Think of a moment in your childhood where you realized something was wrong and explain how you felt.

2.   What was your thought process that led you to conclude that something was wrong?

3.   What is the benefit for receiving an appetizer (being a child) as you prepare for the next meal (stage of life)?

FINISH THESE SENTENCES:

1.   My childhood was _________________.

2.   During my childhood I struggled with _________________.

3.   During my childhood I enjoyed _________________.

4.   The purpose of recognizing how your childhood impacts your adulthood is _________________.

5.   I know that I have accepted and moved on from my childhood when _________________.

6.   The purpose of recognizing how your childhood impacts your adulthood is _________________.

SCRIPTURES A-D:

A- All have sinned and fallen short of the Glory of God -Romans 3:23

B- Believe on the Lord Jesus Christ, and thou shall be saved – Acts 16:31

C- Children, obey your parents in the Lord: for this is right. – Ephesians 6:1

D- Depart from evil and do good. – Psalm 34:14

CHAPTER TWO

SOUP

THE LIFE OF TEENS
"THE HEAT IS SERVED"

This is a liquid type of dish that is typically served extremely hot. During this stage of life most teens are piping hot, however once they explore life, the pressures subside a bit. Just like the soup, there comes a point when life cools down when it starts to settle. I remember when I was a little girl how my mom always gave me a birthday party. We had a known family rule that on your birthday you do absolutely nothing but celebrate and whatever else your heart desires. That meant my brother and sister had to do my part of the chores for that day. That was the best part of my day, because I was free to do nothing but have fun. My mom always made it very special for me. There was one birthday that I remember well. I had just turned 15 years old and two of my besties planned a party with my mom for me. During the celebration, the girls told me how they had to plot for me to leave the house. They tricked me into going with them to our neighborhood park because some girls were trying to fight them. Now, I am not a fighter, but when it comes to someone that I care about I will stand up for them if necessary. I got dressed and was headed to take care of business. When we arrived at the park no one was there. I looked at my friends and was like, "where are the people who were trying to fight you?" My friends told me, "maybe they were scared and left." I told them that we should just head back to my house because I did not want mama to think I was going to be gone too long because it was my birthday, and they agreed. When we arrived at my house, I told my friends that I had to go and put some more clothes on. After I got dressed I went back into the living room and all I could hear was, "Surprise!" I was totally shocked and happy all at the same time.

Seeing all the love in the room just for me was priceless! I also remember a time in my teenage years when I went out on my first date. It was my 16th birthday and it was with the love of my life.

When I got to school I received a card, a teddy bear, and special attention all day from him. It was a wonderful day. Later that evening I received balloons and we went to one of our favorite restaurants, then ended up at a beautiful place at the park. I have so many memories as a teenager that were exciting for me. I had a friend from school that I shared a lot of time with. We did everything together. Whenever our school had a dance we went to it; we were inseparable. I never stayed home as a teenager. I was always hanging out at her house and on every Friday our outing was the laundry mat with her mom. Afterward, we went to eat at a local chicken spot. I always ordered the same thing: a breast and a cherry soda. I looked forward to going every weekend and it got to a point that my mom would say, "do you live with me anymore?" My friend and I did everything together, but as we got older we drifted apart because our interests changed. I am not a judgmental person, but I had to make a decision that was best for me. I love her to this day and have always wished the best for her, but part of the process of growing up is learning who you are as an individual and following your own path.

The life of a teen is everything to them. It is a time when most people identify who they are and what they like by focusing on their physical, emotional, sexual, spiritual, and intellectual development and experiences. Physical and hormonal changes may lead to an emotional awareness. Those experiences can cause psychological, health, and social problems to happen in a person's life if not addressed properly.

Most of the time we live our lives just going through the motions and not really embracing the beauty of being a human being because of all the things that we go through. We are not taught how to truly sit back and treasure who we are and what we can do, be, and have. I want to help you to think in a new way that will make you smile instead of being a person that is consumed by problems. If we seek understanding of what happened to us as teens and if it has anything to do with things we go through as adults, it could bring much-needed clarity and healing. Life is more than problems and most teens live their life with a carefree mindset and without worry until things start to happen based on what they have heard, seen, smelled, touched, and possibly even tasted. It is time for us to understand that what we experience is not meant to harm us, instead it is intended to teach us about life and how to handle it. I want us to think about why our Creator graced us to have those five senses and learn how to appreciate them and feel better about it. We need all these components to be able to enjoy this earth. We use them at any given moment of the day and do not even realize it. The way we operate and function helps us to live and do the things we do. We have a lot to learn about the senses because hearing, seeing, smelling, touching, and tasting give us important information. Most of the time we are affected by what we see and hear. What we see influences how we make decisions even when we do not realize it. Think about a time when you may have seen or heard any type of abuse. Even though you might not have been the one defiled, that does not dismiss the fact that you witnessed it and were damaged by it. You may have internalized it, causing you to have a distorted view of life. It is stored in your thought process because you saw it.

It's the same thing with hearing. I remember as a little girl hearing, "sticks and stones may break my bones, but words will never hurt me." Adults used this for the purpose of reversing our psychology to console us and condition us not to listen to hurtful things. However, it did not change the impact of certain words on how I felt about myself. Words are designed to make you or break you. Loving words will encourage a person and harsh words discourage. I was created with the ability to have feelings and I should have been able to express them without being told that words should not matter. Words can hurt and if you are a sensitive person that is a very important part of how you process things. It is based on what is said and how it is said. Nothing is wrong with being a sensitive person and if the truth be told, your gender has nothing to do with it. A man has the right to feel hurt by words too.

I should have been able to speak on what I had heard if it caused me pain. I wish I would have been told, "Yes words may hurt, but you do not have to accept them." I needed to know how to handle hurtful words in a way that did not break me. If you are like me, your response may not be a strong enough comeback when someone is speaking unkind words. I should have been taught how to communicate with people who used unkind words. We are sometimes affected more by what someone says than by what was done. For instance, it is possible that sticks and stones could hurt, but more than likely it will not be a lingering type of hurt. Words can have a more long lasting and intensely impactful position in our lives. As I became more confident in myself, the words of others were not as important anymore. I learned that hurt people, hurt people and that words are their weapon.

I remember having a conversation with someone very dear to me one day. We both love to work out and, on that day, we decided to take a walk in the neighborhood. I could tell that the person was dealing with something, but I wanted to be patient and respectful without appearing forceful. Right at the end of our workout was when I spoke up and assured the person that I was there to be a listener. As they opened up to me about some things, I found myself talking to them about who we are as humans and that caused us to get into a very deep conversation about our sensory abilities as people. The energy and level of our conversation was so powerful that I could feel the chains falling off the person. I told them not to minimize who they were by maximizing the situation that they were dealing with to the point that it caused them to feel hopeless.

If that resonates with you, it is time for you not to be driven by what you see and what you hear. We can set ourselves free emotionally by understanding what our triggers are. We do not have to live a dysfunctional life anymore because we are learning how to manage our emotions. We must stop ourselves from moving backward and begin moving forward. As I shared with my friend, the painful things you've witnessed are in your past now. You don't have to punish yourself because of what you've seen and heard. If you were exposed to harmful things as a child that you were not mature enough to handle, forgive the adults who did not protect you the way they should have.

It is time for you to experience life from a position of hope. We must free ourselves from the wounds of our childhood and become mature adults. That conversation with my friend was so healing for the both of us because we started to remove the layers of pain and began building a route that was newly established. Today, as I reflect on my childhood it is more of a release than a burden. What I had to experience in my past, is no different than what I experience today. I am just seeing it through a new lens now. My new lens shows me peace instead of pain. Look through your own lens. If what you see is not healthy, not effective, and brings more trouble instead of opportunity, then deal with it, process it, and let it go. We look to other people to free us, but we must be the first to break the chains and release the past. We are the ones who matter the most. Make the first step to live a new life. Let your Creator bring His healing and His warm embracing power. Stop being a person who rejects what the anointing is trying to do in your life. Set yourself free. Live in the present and not the past! Let your Creator show you His beautiful patience and power. Once I did this I knew that I did not have to resist where I was in my life because of where I thought I should be. The things we go through are simply chapters in our life, not the complete book of our life story. Our story will end when we leave this earth, but the legacy will still live on and until then it is time to live and not die. Do not give up on you, keep striving, keep pressing, and moving forward in the power that is in you. Do not be discouraged by what you see or hear anymore. Now is the time to live life with your sixth sense that tells you to walk by faith. This sense will cause you to have hope, it will give you a revelation of newness and power. You will walk in a new layer of skin. The five senses that our Creator gave us are beautiful and needed, but our sixth sense is our faith. It sets us free! We must grab hold of it and enjoy it.

There is a process of discovering and developing the sixth sense and a crucial part of this development is the teenage years. My teenage life started out like any other. I experienced physical changes that were very different for me. I did not have guidance with that from my parents. I did not know that everyone goes through changes with their body, mind, and emotions. I think many parents believe that children should figure things out own their own, but really parents are the ones who should be the first to pre-pare a child for the unknown. I am not saying this to bash anyone (including myself), because there are things they may not realize they needed to prepare their child for. What I mean is that when boys go through things physically, a mother may not even know how to help or prepare them because they are not males and could not possibly know what to do or say. I know that I was not the best in this area, because I was clueless as to what my boys were experiencing. If you are a mom and were not there for your son in the way he needed as he was experiencing bodily changes, it really is okay, you likely did not know you needed to be there for him in that way. Maybe you can find a strong male to spend time with your son(s) and help them understand what their physical body is going through (if one is not there). It is not a bad thing, it is a human thing.

For me, I did not know that my physical changes were attractive to guys and that opened a whole new world for me. My mom was there, but absent when it came to explaining the stages that I was going to become familiar with. I am a very shy person, so I truly struggled with sharing or asking about personal things like bodily changes. My body matured very fast and by the time I was thirteen, I was attracting men well above my age. The compliments were appreciated, but I was very mindful not to allow my body image to get me into situations that I could not handle. My body was changing, and I had to learn how to embrace it and not be afraid, so I thought! I remember going through childhood crushes, but not fully understanding what all of that meant. My parents did not approve of me dating until I was around 16, but that did not stop me from talking to guys and being interested in what they thought about me.

I was not one who explored a lot of guys, but there was one who I was truly fond of and I did not know how to handle those emotions. I met him when I was in the second grade and had butterflies in my stomach whenever I saw him, but because I was a "chubby" little girl he paid me no attention. As I got a little older, I was still intrigued by this fellow. I remember we had a class party in the fifth grade, and I asked my mom if we could go shopping, because I needed an outfit for the party. I remember I picked out this off-white turtleneck sweater with a brown corduroy skirt to go with my brown shoes. Mama did my hair and she even allowed me to wear some lip gloss. I was super excited and could not sleep the night before the dance. I could not wait for him to see me. Well, I got to school the next day, and guess what? He did not even notice me at all. It was as though I was this invisible person. Not only did he not pay me any attention, no one in my class said anything about my "new look". All I wanted to do was find some food and eat, and after I did that I went into the bathroom and cried. I remembered looking in the mirror, saying his name, and telling him that one day he will ask me on a date and I will say NO. I laugh about it today, because eventually, that did happen. Finally, one day the guy that I was trying to get attention from genuinely noticed me. He even actually spoke to me. He came up to me and we had a basic conversation and everything. You know I was shocked right? But, instead of enjoying that moment it really annoyed me and I immediately lost interest in him. I guess it was because he had only noticed me after my major weight loss.

A while had passed and by the time I was fifteen he had gotten enough courage to ask me to go out on a date. I told him my parents did not allow me to date and I had an overprotective brother who no one wanted to mess with, but that did not stop this guy. He was persistent. One day I was eating lunch with one of my besties and he came up to me at the lunch table and asked, "Do you like my shoes?" I looked at him like, "Really dude, you are seriously asking me do I like your shoes?" It was hilarious to my friend and I but guess what? At that moment, my feelings came back and I remembered why I loved him so much. He was the cutest, funniest, most entertaining guy you could possibly lay your eyes on and he actually liked me. When we looked at each other it was magical, and the chemistry was strong between us. I was shocked and infatuated with his attention. We started dating and grew very fond of each other. It was hard dating one of the most popular guys in high school, but because of my love for him I dealt with all that came with it. I had so many enemies and did not understand why at the time. I was so in love with him and there was nothing that I would not do for him. Every morning before going to school I used my allowance to buy him breakfast. I gave him everything and it was not because he asked. He never did that. I always just wanted to show him how much he meant to me. I now realize that I did not show him that I needed that same type of care. I was so busy pleasing him to the point that I never learned who I was or what I liked, so when he did ask I was clueless with my response. At that point he was giving and doing things that he thought I would like because I did not tell him otherwise. I just was accepting what he thought was best for me. I had no idea of who I was and what I wanted. That was not his fault at all. I was driven by what others thought I should have because of my lack of awareness for myself. I didn't even have a desire to find out what I wanted and how to make it happen. Now I realize that it is important to invest in yourself first before you try to pour into someone else.

Anyway, one day my sweet fairytale was interrupted when I found out about his unfaithfulness in our relationship. I discovered a lot of things that I just did not want to hear about. What I thought was the best thing in my life at the time, ended up being one of the hardest things I had to deal with. Not only was I too young for this type of relationship, I eventually found out I was going to be a teenage mom. I was having a child with a guy who clearly was not ready to be with only me. As I think about it today, why would he? We were two young people just getting to know ourselves, but during this stage of life we were acting on our out-of-control hormones and ended up facing an adult lifestyle way too early. I remembered the day that I had to tell him and my parents that I was pregnant. I was devastated, because I knew that we were not in a good place and I did not want him to be upset with me or think I was going to interrupt his sports plans. It was the hardest thing for me to do and I just could not believe that I was going to be a parent. To my surprise he was very supportive and never made me feel like he did not want to have a child with me. That took so much pressure off me and gave me the courage to tell my parents. I told my mom and asked her to share it with my dad because I was afraid of what he would do to me. Even their reactions were a surprise. My mom was very supportive, and she showed me love and never made me feel bad about being a teen mother. Really, we became closer than we ever had been before. She was not ashamed of what her family or friends thought. It was a good feeling having that type of kindness shown. What I thought would be the worst news that a mother could hear from her child ended up being one of the most supportive gestures of love that I could have experienced. Mama never judged me, and to this day she loves my son to pieces. I remember her telling me that she would be there with me through it all and she was. For that, I vowed to take my role as a parent very seriously.

Mama gave me a baby shower and was there for me during my delivery. She never left my side with anything that I had to face as a new parent. The dad and I were no longer a couple, but that did not stop him for being there for his son. He and his family helped me with our son and he never missed a moment during his early childhood. I love his family to this very day and I appreciate all that each one of his family members did for me and our child. As time passed and maturity settled in, eventually he became my husband. We later had three more children together. However, my life was affected by the decisions that I made as a teenager.

As I reflect on things now, psychologically, I was in overdrive. Here I was, a pregnant teenager, who didn't even know how to make decisions for herself, let alone a child. I did not know that my life would have been molded into such an image. Due to my body changing so much during my pregnancy, I had developed some health issues that caused me to be socially removed from my peers. I did not graduate with my original classmates. I was very determined to earn my diploma, so after I had my son I went back to school and finished my education at another school during the summer.

Your life as a teen may not be like my story, but I know you have a story and when you think about it you may find out that the things that were happening during that time may have impacted your adult choices. My teenage life was very difficult. I made adult decisions from a place of immaturity, even though in our society a person is considered an adult at the age of 18. I still do not understand that status being granted for a person who must depend on others to provide for them. This can cause a lot of confusion for a teen because they can argue that they are "grown" and can be very disrespectful to their parent's authority. I blame that on society (adults) because they have deposited that mindset into the teens mind and that is why most of us struggled morally, socially, and emotionally. The power of a teenager is extremely strong because they can be rebellious, fiery, demanding, controlling, caring, and loving all at the same time. Those traits are the life and behavior of many teens and if not handled correctly, those types of behaviors will just continue to operate and grow with us as adults.

Now is the time for us to identify these behaviors to completely get free from those reactions if you are ready. During this stage of life, we make heated off track (hot) decisions that can get us into a lot of uncomfortable situations like mine did for me. Think about soup for a moment. It is hot when first serving it and then it will cool down the longer it is left out. We can be just like that as people - we have a fiery hot side then eventually we learn how to cool down and not react so emotionally. If you are a person who usually reacts emotionally, maybe it is time for you to reflect and find a better way to handle situations. It is time to learn how to appreciate, value, and treasure people and handle situations in a calmer, more peaceful way. This may take some time because you may not be used to it. Often, the first thing we think about when we are ready for change is to look for a person to help instead of digging deep and discovering how you can get help from the One who created you and knows you better than you know yourself.

He knew us from the time we were in our mother's womb. He is the only One who can help us see things the way He does. God can change the way we think and live if we allow Him to. You may not have realized that as a teenager, but if you are ready you can start a new way of living and thinking. We must learn the spiritual part of who we are and connect with our Creator daily. He will teach us how to stop having adult tantrums and show us how to stop blowing up. He is the one Who will diffuse us if we allow Him to. It is time to turn off the teenager and turn on the adult way of handling life situations. I think all of us have experienced intense and exhausting events, and now we are learning how to handle them without becoming a time bomb. The goal is not to allow a spirit of rebelliousness to overtake us anymore and learn to be more listeners than responders.

Have you ever tried to find out what triggers your mindset to react in an unhealthy way? Think about this part of your life for a moment. Did you see and hear things as a young person that could have caused you to develop habits and patterns that were not good for you? Did you experience any suicidal thoughts or were you ever influenced to try drugs? When were you exposed to sexuality and immoral views? All these questions are asked to set your mind, spirit, and soul free. It is time for you to realize that what you experienced influences your choices and views of today. Once you make the connection you will discover that it was during a time in your life where things for humans start to heat up. I want you to examine what happened to you so that you can now get the support that you need if you feel like it is still trying to control you. You may not be that person you were as a teen anymore, but you do need to see where it all started for you. I say that so you can begin to say to yourself, "I am not that person anymore, that was a younger me who was trying to figure things out." It is time for you to stop responding in an impulsive, childish way. I know that if you are or have dealt with substance abuse it is not that easy to release it, but you can get yourself the help that you need if you are ready to move forward with a new and improved you. Your teenage experiences introduced you to those things, but as an adult you can let it go! It is up to you and hopefully you won't allow rebelliousness to settle in. We have the power within to remove any form of it if we want to start being more optimistic about our situations. That type of energy is not a crime, but it is damaging if it is not controlled. The way we respond to situations can be dangerous for us. When I think about rebelliousness, my mind goes to the place of a person who strongly desires attention and if they do not get it they will channel their energy to a place of defiance. I thought about this very hard and realized that the problem is "identity". As people we want to feel and know that we matter and if we are feeling threatened by a lack of attention our emotions start to kick in and then we may appear arrogant and say we do not care. I always hear people say they do not care when something important happens to them. It is like when those words are released, it covers the truth that they really *do* care, but it makes them feel vulnerable to admit it. I do not think we want people to see that type of energy, but the truth is we all have it in us.

Our goal now is to identify problem behavior and attack it. When I became a mother, it was clearer for me how childhood experiences shaped long-term behavior. Having already raised three out of four children during the adolescent stage, I observed that rebellion resulted when my children didn't receive something they thought they should have. As a parent, I knew that I had to sacrifice a lot for the sake of my children. That worked in my favor, because they did not have many experiences that caused them to rebel. I truly have four amazing children. Yes, they are human and have gone through a lot in life, especially having to be raised in a single parent home, but we shared a lot that helped when adversity started in their lives. When I think of the love and pain a parent will go through for their child it always reminds me of the Creator's purpose in sending Jesus and helping us to understand what an ultimate sacrifice really is. So, as I understand the cause of rebelliousness I understand even more the purpose behind it. Since Jesus died on the cross and forgave us of our sins (mistakes), I knew I had to also forgive my children. None of us asked to be on this earth and all of us are learning every day. As parents we want our children to think we have everything under control, but I have learned that it is better for me to be transparent with my children so that they know they are not experiencing anything that I did not. Our Creator has already told us that "There is nothing new under the sun" (Ecclesiastes 1:9). Therefore, any emotion we deal with, God already has a word for us to speak over it and receive deliverance. Generations and eras will change, but there is no issue of life that has not happened before.

I have often heard parents say, "When my child turns 18 they have to leave home, I have raised them." In a way, that could make a person feel like they have been abandoned and they must figure everything out. That is a hard thing to do if you have not been truly directed and prepared for this dysfunctional world. We should hold young people accountable, but we can still guide them along the way. I can only imagine where I would be if I did not have my parents' support during my decision of having a child so young. They did not throw me out; I had support. Well maybe you did not have that type of support, and now you realize why you could be having a rebellious energy when it comes to dealing with things. It is time that you receive encouragement so that you can have a healthier lifestyle. It is time for you to be able to communicate effectively and not driven by any energy other than understanding your path. As an adult we can see more clearly as to why we respond the way we do. We do not have to dismiss our teenage experiences however, we do have to understand how they have been influencing us. I know that most of us want to be heard, and if someone is not paying attention to our views, we get mad about it. I had to be a person who truly followed this principle that God gave to us when we feel that way. He said for us to be, "Swift to listen and slow to speak" (Psalms 15:1). When I was a teen, I always defended myself when I felt insulted or offended. I would react very quickly if I felt like someone questioned my actions. I always had a guard up when I was around people and I know a lot of it had to do with my insecurity with my weight and from my upbringing. I consistently heard conversations that sounded like arguments all the time. Therefore, I became that person, but inside I really did not want to be.

I wanted to be a peaceful, calm, and understanding person, but I did not know how to become that person. I was constantly getting frustrated by everything until one day I had an encounter with my Creator and He showed me myself. He told me the truth about why I behaved that way. I had to reflect a lot on what caused me to have those feelings. One major reason was I wanted others to do things like me and when they had their own ideas and plans it made me feel like they had a problem with what I was doing. I had to learn it was okay for others not to see things from my prospective, because I did not always see or do things that others were requesting of me. I was not operating with the mindset that people have their own opinions and it really is okay if they do not agree with me. I knew that frustration only happened when it was not going my way. Ouch! I was feeding my ego and enjoying it, although my spirit was screaming for me to be more flexible with others. I was not raised to follow my spirit, instead I was shown how to fight for what I wanted and that was it. Another reason why I was so frustrated was because I wanted to be accepted as well. All I really wanted was to be supported and I took it personally. I was beyond doubt warring with myself because I did not always show how I was really feeling outwardly. It is important to be aware of what triggers us to operate that way.

We must realize that there is a war going on inside of us and we must overcome it. As teenagers we usually do not get that consciousness unless we have learned it from someone who recognizes what spiritual warfare is and helps us to distinguish that the best weapon is the Word of God. This is such a powerful gift that God has blessed us with if we operate in it and teach our children how to operate in it when they are in this phase of life. We must understand that being in the presence of God is all the power we need to deal with our life issues. The bottom line is we have a soul and we have a purpose to fulfill in our Creator, but if we are not taught that then we will feel that we are facing circumstances alone. I know we have all ambled through life feeling defeated at times, however, we must understand that life is full of lessons for us to learn and one of them is knowing who we are in Christ. God will teach us how to walk with strong morals and learn how to resist our own insecurities.

I am excited for new ways of thinking about life as we walk on a new path toward healing. Our five senses are a blessing and we must understand that they are not a curse nor intended to damage us. If no one has ever told you they were sorry for exposing you to things that you were not ready to handle, I will say it for them, "I am sorry." It is time for you to start to meditate on things that will lift your spirits and not tear you down. You now understand that people used to harm you because you allowed it, but now you know how to shut down negative energy. Cease to feed into the lies and rebuke words and actions that are not intended to build you up. When you see things that concern you, don't allow it to consume you to the point that you feel paralyzed and cannot function. It is time to take control of your senses and live with a clear and peaceful purpose. You can embrace what you see as a point in your life to gain a better awareness and if it is something that you do not want to do, you will be more willing to remove yourself versus trying to find a way to accept it. Our vision is a gift from our Creator. Begin to love all the gifts that your Creator gave you because they are your navigation to a beautiful place. Yes, your past may have been hard, but it was because the people who shared that time with you didn't protect you the way they should have. Everyone was directed differently, but now you can help yourself and the next generation to stop the cycle of living life without love, support, and hope. We are learning how to put to rest what needs to be detached from us and awaken what we need to live for, now. It is time to stop allowing your teenage experiences to dictate and run your adult life. Treasure the memories that you need to, and if there are any that bring you pain, it is time to say goodbye to them! We must release those behaviors because we have now outgrown them. I will always love my journey as a teenager, but that time has passed, and I must be fully developed so that I can understand my next phase with a view of freedom. It is time to live a healthier, optimistic life. When I think about the five senses and what they mean to me, I can sum it up best like this, "There is nothing as comforting in my life nor sweeter, loving, giving, touching, and peaceful as when I call on the Name of Jesus in prayer" (–LWB Beckwith). I have a new mind since I am determined to "Wake up every day with a goal to go out in the world and mastermind it with positivity." –LWB Beckwith

MASTERMIND

1. As a teenager, whose approval were you seeking? What things did you do or say to gain that approval?

2. Think about or describe a time when you were dissatisfied with the process of gaining other people's approval.

3. What influences trigger you to question your identity now?

4. How have you learned to cool down the soup (pressures of life)?

FINISH THESE SENTENCES:

1. We should constantly encourage ourselves to not to continue to ________________________________

    ________________________________.

2. I will work toward not allowing myself to

    ________________________________.

3. I have learned that being a teenager has

    ________________________________.

SCRIPTURES E – H:

E – Even a child is known by his doings. – Proverbs 20:11

F – Fear not: for I am with thee. – Isaiah 43:5

G – God is love. – I John 4:8

H – Honor thy father and thy mother. – Exodus 20:12

CHAPTER THREE

SALAD

*"Learn to take a COOL approach after your
LOVE has been awakened."*

YOUNG ADULTS

This dish is served cold and has various mixtures and/or dressings to make it more flavorful. During the developmental stage young adults need a mixture of good healthy choices to help them cope with life issues in a healthy way. Who am I? What do I want to do with my life? What is my purpose? Why do I need to start making decisions for myself now? These are all questions that go through a young adults' mind. I grappled with these questions as a young adult, while also having someone else depending on me for their life. I did not really know myself and then I had the full-time responsibility of nurturing and taking care of another being. I had a seed that relied on me.

I will share my story and how powerful every step was to me. I have always been a person who relied on what others thought I should do instead of what I thought. In my family, I was the one who just seemed like I always needed someone to direct my steps. Maybe it was because I was quiet and did not speak on things like others did. I was, and am, an observer. I do not speak on what I do not know, and I do not do what I have not learned. When I started making decisions for myself, others questioned them as though they were not good enough. It may have been because I did not seek their advice. When people approached me with their opinions, I second-guessed myself and what I wanted to do. I made decisions based on others and not necessarily on what I wanted. I was living with my mom when I had my son and I remember saying to myself, "I need to make some changes in my life because I am a mother now." I did not know what that looked like, but I knew I had to do something different. I had to make major changes after becoming a mother at such a young age. I had to become independent from my parents whether I wanted to or not. My mom did not mind me and my son living with her, but I just felt the need to live on my own and raise my son to the best of my ability. So, I decided to go out and look for an apartment. What was amazing about my hunt for a place for myself and my son was that I ended up going back to the neighborhood that I grew up in. I was familiar with it and felt very good about it. I went and got an application, filled it out, and paid the application fee. Once I was approved, I had to pay a deposit. I had a really good job at a local university and I knew that I would be able to afford the rent. In the meantime, I kept working, providing for my son, and living at home with my mom. One day I received the call that forever changed my life from depending on my mom to being independent. I got the apartment!

I was overjoyed, excited, nervous, and scared all at the same time. I knew that my life was shifting in a new direction. I had to sit back and figure out how I was going to handle all this responsibility that I had now. Typically, during this time most young adults choose to live with their relatives as long as possible, but I was not that typical person anymore. I had to discover how to take care of myself and my child's needs, desires, ambitions, and goals without help and support from my parents. That was extremely scary for me because I did not know what that looked like.

I always had my parents. I was willing to let all that go because I knew it was time for me to grow up. I could have stayed with my parents, but I would have been very unhappy, and I could possibly have taken it out on them. I knew that I could not allow my condition of living with them hinder me from what I knew was best for me as a young adult. Instead of me going away to school I was going away with a child and facing the reality of the real world alone. I had to jump into the real world with no hesitation. I made the decision to move out and free myself from depending on my mom because I had someone who depended on me. I felt like that would be better for me and her. At this point in a person's life it can feel like you are too old to be at home, and too young to survive alone (at least that was the case for me). I did not want my mother to dictate my life based on hers and I did not want her trying to be my son's mother and have him respect her more than me. I knew I was not quite ready to be on my own either, so it was very hard to make that decision. I discovered that it was not as easy as I originally thought. I really was not ready for the responsibility that I had put myself in, and I had no other choice but to face what I had done. It was very scary for me to have had the thought of moving out into the world and becoming a full-time mom, worker, and independent individual. Many young adults are just not ready for what society calls "independence". We think they are because they "look" prepared. Many leave high school heading to college, which some may feel is the best way to discover independence, while still having some dependency on their parents. That was not the case for me. I did finish high school, but college was nowhere near my focus at that time. One reason was, I did not see that lifestyle within my home. No one in my family talked about college let alone trying to apply to one, so, I did not factor that into my plans. I only saw my parents going to work and providing for us daily, so that was my goal for myself and my child as well. It is amazing how we model after our parents and do not even realize it. At that time in my life, I did not know what other options were out there for me other than being a provider for my son and myself. All I knew was that it was time for me to take a deep breath, hold my shoulders back, and move in the direction of living an independent life. I was not leaving home to run away, instead I was ready to see what life had to offer a young mom with a child. I had no other reason to leave home. My mom was not pressuring me to leave, and truth be told, she was totally hurt when I left. She did not want me to leave and if I did not have my son I probably would have stayed right there. I love her and appreciated her support, but I knew it was time. I had to become fully responsible for my actions.

I cannot believe I had so much strength at such a young age. A "young adult" is just a teenager, stepping from one era of life into another. Being young just means being in the first stages of life and growing in responsibility. At this point in life most people are inexperienced and possibly immature. We transition into adulthood so quickly and sometimes skip important steps in the process of developing maturely. If you were a young adult who had to figure things out alone, it is ok. That part of life is called trial and error. We all have experienced it at some point. Back in my time, leaving home showed responsibility, plus most parents told their children that they had to leave home and do something with their lives. It was very important for me to help my young adult children to not rush their transitions in life, to become fully aware of what they needed to do as individuals, and not feel defeated by this world and the things that come with it.   I wanted them to fully understand what I had to do because of the choices that I had made. I had to learn how to take care of myself. When you are living on your own, you learn how to manage a home, how to manage your finances, and how to take care of other things in life for which you were dependent on your parents earlier. Living independently can bring a lot of growth as we all know. It is a hard time for most people because we are still discovering ourselves. It is hard to process the fact that you leave one stage of life where everything is given to you, and now you are entering a stage in life where you must provide for yourself. It is like going from one extreme to another. How do you figure all of this out and keep yourself together? During this point most people just react to the change and don't fully understand it or think too deeply and become paralyzed to the point that they just do nothing.

If you can relate to any of that, now is the time to reflect on who you are and what you want for your life now. You do not have to be, nor feel, stuck. You may be realizing why you operate the way you do. It may be a possibility that you can release any disappointments you experienced during this stage and enter a new era of thinking for your life. It is time to analyze yourself and self-evaluate so you can live in peace with who you are and where your habits came from. We need to work on coming out of our childhood/young adult stage and really be okay with it as we move forward and grow older. I know this may be a hard pill to swallow for some people. For example, my daughter really loved her childhood and she shared with me that her experience was so memorable that she did not want to grow-up. I am glad she experienced a happy childhood, but we have seasons in our lives, and that part of her life was over. Now she must learn how to enjoy her season as a young adult. I know that her emotions may be all over the place, but I would rather she experience the transition now versus becoming a full-grown adult still wishing she was a child. On the other hand, my oldest son rushed his childhood, because he wanted to become an adult and be an independent person. Both can be unhealthy if you do not allow yourself time to go through the entire process of maturity. My middle son did not want to stay a child, but he was confused as to how a young adult should respond to life issues. He did not know how it looked and that caused him to deal with things very emotionally. If we allow our feelings to drive us, we can be all over the place. Young adults experience all types of emotions such as frustration, being overwhelmed, and disappointed. All these feelings can be very challenging to deal with as they transition into independence. Think about frustration for a moment. It is a reaction to a situation that a person feels is out of their hands and are not really equipped to handle. For instance, a baby, who is trying to walk and gets frustrated when they keep falling. They cry and feel sad for a moment but then the parent encourages them again to get up and continue trying. That is how God is with adults who are still soul searching. He gently tells us to rethink some things with His guidance so that we can do things differently. The baby tries again, more cautiously until they gain confidence. Young adults are the same way. They must slow down and take one step at a time. Life is a process and our society does not do a good job with displaying that.

Are you happy with how your life is right now? If so, great, and if not, take a moment to step back and reevaluate things by analyzing them. Then, start moving in the direction that you want to see improvement in. I remember a moment when my son was helping me put some mulch down in front of our house. I watched him from afar and I was truly amazed by what I saw. He first sat down on the ground and studied the area. Then he pulled up everything that was there and started fresh by cleaning up the area and lining the bricks up correctly. Next, he put the plastic down, and placed the mulch where it needed to have gone. It was great to see how he just did not dump the new mulch on top of the old.

In life we get frustrated because we are trying to change our environment instead of changing ourselves. It only causes us to become afraid and frustrated. Then, that energy can cause us to start fearing things. Most of the time we are simply being led by the spirt of fear and do not even realize it. We do not have to fear the unknown, we just have to be willing to try the unknown and make it known. The struggle for independence for young people is real, therefore parents really should prepare their children for this part of life. As a parent we automatically make decisions for our children and when the time comes for them to leave, they may be struggling with their independence. Life can be overwhelming if the young adult does not feel prepared when having to start thinking for themselves. For me, it was just understood that I had to do what I did. I was not guided into this stage, but once I entered it, I had to make things happen. Being independent does not mean you cannot get advice from people, it simply means that you are solely responsible for the choices that you make. Most of us were not taught how to function in this world. We were only told we had to do it and figure it out. I personally do not think that is fair because life is so broad and general and without the proper guidelines set in place how are we to carry things out without struggling and feeling defeated most of the time? It is hard to figure out things that we did not create. If I created a car, then I should know how to operate it, but if *you* create that car I must trust you to tell me how it should run. For a person to want the car they will have to rely on the experiences of others and know that "if they made it through, then so can I". It will all come together. Life is a big puzzle and we must put our own story map together.

Young adults must learn how to be mature people very early especially when they make choices like moving out, getting married, having children, and taking on debt like credit cards, making major purchases like cars, etc. Education on these topics should not be withheld from any child because in time they will be a young adult. I struggled with feeling like I could have prepared my children a little better in these areas, but they tell me that I did a good job. When parents teach their children about these decisions it will not be so overwhelming or detrimental to them. There is still a lot of developmental growth that happens during this phase, so it would be wise to learn how to make these types of big decisions during this time and not when you get too much older. Life is intended for us to enjoy ourselves in a healthy and wholesome way. It is hard to face some of the things that come with it, but we must keep trying.

I love the Serenity Prayer, "God grant me the serenity to accept the things I cannot change and the courage to change the things I can." We cannot change others, but we can change ourselves. This quote put everything into perspective for me. I know that if a young adult can receive this message, they will feel more liberated to live and not feel defeated. Unfortunately, some children are forced to grow up too fast. I have spoken with a lot of children who had to take on adult responsibilities at a very young age. Being a certain age doesn't make you qualified to deal with certain things. Most often, those children end up resenting all that responsibility that an adult should have had. Sometimes as an adult they are living with a childlike mentality because they had to be an adult during the childhood season of their life. I loved the feedback that Erik Erikson focused on regarding the way we think. He was a psychologist and psychoanalyst who was known for his theory of the psychological development of human beings. He shared the importance of children experiencing each growth phase in the correct order for them to truly be effective individuals. Everyone's situation is different, but everyone should understand the natural process. For instance, some people can get married at 18 and it be the right choice, while some can get married at 30 and it be the wrong choice for them. Either way they made the choice and must deal with it no matter what their age is.

I learned that I could not jump into anything too fast or I would risk the possibility of not being prepared for it. I did not want my children to make the mistakes that I did, so I was trying to be proactive when in turn I was appearing controlling and insensitive to their needs. My intentions were in the right place but got crossed because of misunderstanding. Young people will make mistakes because they are human, but they do not have to feel like their situation is hopeless and they are not loved. I have learned that during this stage we really need to feel loved and we seek after it in so many ways. Most of the time we are looking for it from others. I think that as humans we need to always feel love from another person and it should be shown in more than a physical way. However, I know for most of us we do not think someone loves us unless there is intimacy, and if it is not received then we will isolate ourselves from them and the world. During this stage we have the desire to start seeking love and affection from a person. I am not just referring to sexual needs. We are also seeking love from our family and friends. As people we want to know we are safe and being cared for in a committed way. When these needs are not met, we withdraw. I think that is why so many relationships fail. A person taps out of showing someone love and then they stop caring about how they feel. The other person starts to search for someone else to love and care for them. I was never one to continue to seek love from a person, because I believed that once they got tired of me then they would just remove themselves and I would be left behind and hurt from their decision. I know how it feels to love and not receive it back the way you give it. I had to learn how to identify love and not feel confused about it.

As individuals we want to connect with others and feel valued. We do not like rejection because we were not designed to feel or be rejected. So, when this emotion happens to us we shut down or run to someone else to rescue us from what someone else has done. We war against our own egos and to some degree we cause a lot of self-rejection. Just like we want to be and feel loved, we embrace pain just the same. The more we look for love the more pain is right there to take us down. We look for love from people to get us through our difficult moments, but we must rise above that. We must know that we are loved first by our Creator and His love is not com-promising. He loves us no matter what we say or do! When I discovered that I was delivered from having low self-esteem, I no longer felt the need to be loved by man only. I was secure with just knowing that my Creator's love was and is good enough for me. Now, please do not get me wrong. I do need natural love, but if it is not real it will cause me to isolate myself from the world and I am just not willing to do that anymore. Erikson argues that "intimacy has a counterpart: Distantiation is the readiness to isolate if necessary, to destroy those forces and people who, in essence seem dangerous to our own, and whose territory seems to encroach on the intent of one's intimate relations" (1950).

In life, we must take one step at a time. The first step is knowing you are loved by God and then you must love yourself for someone to love you the way you need to be loved. We must identify what we want and need before we can receive it from someone else. I have healed from my past relationship and I am looking forward to whatever is in my future. I will not allow myself to feel nor be isolated anymore. I had to dig deep inside and pull out the little person who did not understand that I needed a different type of love. I am seeking a love that is committed to me. My first true love is within and that will pour out on the one who can handle it. I know that love is more powerful than we want to admit. It is natural to want to receive and give love. If you struggle with loving or being loved it is okay to seek support from a professional. Counseling is not taboo; it is not good to keep yourself sheltered, confused, and dysfunctional all because you did not take the time to get help.

Having a counselor to listen objectively to you will provide a better way to deal with any type of situation. You may have asked yourself questions such as: "How can I be redeemed from bad decisions that I made as a young adult? How is it negatively affecting me now? How do I come back from that? Counseling can be a helpful resource to stop living life in a negative, dysfunctional way. This process will take time, so ask God to allow patience to have her way and guide you into a better head space. I know some people think that counseling is for "crazy people." Instead it is for wise people who are tired of living their lives in a crazy way. It is all in how we perceive things. Learn to take a cool approach after a hot moment!

MASTERMIND

1.   What challenges (emotions) did you face while transitioning into adulthood and independence?

2.   How can you make decisions that are not based on your emotions?

3.   Do you feel that counseling/therapy is necessary when transitioning through different seasons in your life?

4.   How can you be redeemed from negative situations and make a strong comeback?

5.   What does love truly look like to you?

FINISH THESE SENTENCES:

1. My emotions helped me transition when I
    ________________________________.

2. I stopped basing my decisions from my emotions because ________________________.

3. I understand that therapy is ______________
    ________________________________.

4. When I am frustrated I will ______________
    ________________________________.

5. When I make decisions, I will ____________
    ________________________________.

6. Therapy   to   me   means   ____________
    ________________________________.

7. I would rather think positively, not negatively, because ________________________
    ________________________________.

8.   I will show love by ____________________

____________________________________.

SCRIPTURES I-L:

I – I will instruct thee and teach thee in the way which thou shalt go: I will counsel thee with mine eyes upon thee. – Psalms 32:8

J – Jesus saith unto him, I am the way, the truth, and the life: no man cometh unto the Father, but by Me. – John 14:6

K – Keep thy tongue from evil. – Psalm 34:13

L – Look unto Me and be ye saved. – Isaiah 45:22

CHAPTER FOUR

SORBET

It is time to clean your palate and transition from one stage to another. This dish is served with two different purposes. First it is a refresher for your taste buds, and it is purposed to clean/clear the palate for the next course. It has a cool texture to it, and the taste is not too sweet. In life we must be refreshed and learn how to clean/clear our paths by adjusting, emerging, and transitioning into an adult. During this stage, adults are expected to know their goals and should be operating in them. However, some people do not know how to adjust as an adult and struggle with trying to figure things out without overwhelming themselves to a point of giving up. It may appear easier to give up in life and some people do. We all may have come across a person wanting to end their life because it was just too much that they had to deal with. They did not know how to adjust from one thing to another. Therefore, the reality of transitioning from one stage or role into the next may just be too much. I want to say to you today, do not give up on YOU. Find a way to pull yourself out of the pit that you are in or help someone else to pull themselves out. Get into a group with people who had or have common struggles and receive support. We are never alone in this universe and we can always look up something or find someone who can help us. If my book is your helper, great. If you need more support, great. Never stop trying. As adults we must learn how to regulate, and transition into the next phase of life without quitting even when things do not look like they matter or will work out for our benefit. We need to fully understand that when situations happen that is out of our control, it is important to seek help and get some direction, so we won't feel defeated. We should enjoy the fullness of life without struggling mentally, physically, or spiritually all the time. We must adjust our thinking. We need to refresh ourselves in a way that is good for us by merging ourselves with new things and opportunities.

We need to transition our minds from where we are to where we want to be. I had to do that for myself several times once I dealt with the reality that I was a divorced woman. I did not want my marriage to end, but there was nothing I could do to keep it once the decisions were made. I had to deal with it. We all have passion and sometimes it is hard to find a new passion if the one you had has ended for whatever reason. I had to pick myself up from a bad place and create a new life for myself. This process takes time and sometimes we just do not want to wait for it. We want things to change and happen immediately. For me, I wanted things back the way they were, but as I matured and transitioned my thoughts, I realized that those things were not good anyway. I was holding on to something that was weighing me down. I was harming myself emotionally, but I was willing to just stay in it because that is what I thought was best for me. Have you ever felt that way about something? You know it was not good for you, but you wanted to keep it just because that is what you were used to and that is all you had connected yourself with. I eventually discovered that my changes saved my life. I learned how to slow down and prioritize my life so I that could discover all the wonderful things that were in store for me.

Being an adult requires a person to be able to make rational decisions about their emotions, self-interests, moral standards, goals, relationships, plans, and security. I hope you are starting to see how I am trying to make sense of this thing called "life". As an adult I started adjusting and emerged in ways that caused me to identify who I really was. I had moments in my life that I should have discovered sooner about myself but did not because I was more focused on taking care of my children. I remember going to the movies alone for the first time at the age of 30. It was a really uncomfortable, yet necessary venture for me, because I thought those types of moments were supposed to be shared with someone. I was learning how to walk my own path. It was time for me to stop waiting for someone to do something with and for me. I was tired of repeating the same patterns in my life, so going to the movies by myself was so important for me, because I did not know how to meet my own needs and be happy about it.

We all need to discover new things about ourselves and learn to be able to make the changes that we need for our own lives. Breaking free is not easy, but once you do, it truly is a life changer. Another life changing experience for me as an adult was when one of my dear friends that I met when we were in middle school called me one day and invited me to go with her and some of her friends on a beach trip. She knew that I did not go out much and she felt that taking a trip would be a great thing for me to do. However, she also knew I did not like hanging out with people I did not know. I was very skeptical about going, because I never went out overnight with a group of ladies like that before. I did not know how to take time for myself. I have always been focused on being a parent and I totally forgot that I needed some time for myself as well. It is good to have friends who can help you change without it feeling and being forced. I decided to go on the trip and I am glad that I did because I met some wonderful women and that experience truly saved my life in so many ways. I did not know just how much I needed to get away. That trip opened parts of me that I never thought I was dealing with. It is amazing how people can help you change even when you do not think anything needs changing. I learned how to be open with people I did not know, embrace other people's lives and lifestyles without judgement, and just be free to love people for who they are and not what I thought they should be. I did not know that going on that trip was going to be a life changer for me. I never imagined that being surrounded by seven powerful women could change my life in the ways that it did. We all need changes like that for our lives and we do not even know it. Have you ever had a situation you decided to try that became a life changing experience for you? Well, I did and to this very day, I am still hanging with this group of ladies. We were established as the Beach Girls (BG) in 2016 and I am so grateful for my friend who I call "P". She was used by my Creator to help me have a new way of living and looking at life. That change helped me to continue to work toward having a better view of my life and what life truly means to me.

Let me rewind for a moment and talk about my early adulthood experience. I know we all have a learned behavior from our past, but that does not mean we have to keep having that mindset nor living the way we were raised. I was beginning to adjust my life in a way that was beneficial. I was emerging into a new and improved person, and I had to transition from the way my parents raised me and become more aware of who I was and what I wanted. I was ready to be grown mentally and learn how to stop depending on others and my emotions. In doing that, I knew that I had to establish some housekeeping rules. It was time to cleanse my mind of unhealthy thoughts and learn how to embrace the next chapters in my life without feeling like I was doing something wrong.

As an adult, I had to get to a point where I stopped allowing bitterness from past experiences to block me from the sweetness that life has to offer. "In order to get to where you are going, you must learn how to walk away from what you know is not good for you anymore," LWB Butterfly. To get cleansed from my past thoughts I had to attract new thoughts, people, and situations that would support my desire to create a better lifestyle. I was living a stagnated life and wanted things to change. It was important for me to start making my life count. Yes, I was a wife before and a mother, but there was more to me that I had to find out about. I had to learn how to adjust myself from being a mom all the time. I was so focused on that, that I was missing so much of who Lisa was. I had to ask myself some personal questions about who I was and what I desired. It took me a long time to answer them, because I never thought about myself long enough to ask myself anything before. I was so busy trying to properly guide my children in life that I missed out on equipping myself. I discovered so much about myself and never thought that I could do all the things that I later accomplished. I had an opportunity to go to college in my mid-thirties. That was a dream come true, because I never thought I would earn my degree. I was not a very high-level learner in school and I allowed that to lower my self-esteem. While I was a senior in undergrad, God spoke to me and reminded me that I had always wanted to be a teacher. My undergraduate degree was in business, but I decided to get a graduate degree in education. I was happy to finally be pursuing a career path that mattered to me. I had sacrificed for the sake of my children for so long that it felt funny when I started doing things for myself. I do not regret for one moment devoting time and energy to my children, because I witnessed all their development. I had to be there for them as they faced major and minor situations in their own life. I knew deep down that one day I would fulfill my desires once my children were raised, and when the time came for me to do that I truly absorbed every moment of it. It is not good to ignore yourself and I knew I had to start giving myself some attention. I had to learn how to put myself first and how to say no without being rude about it. I started adulthood very early, so I had to figure out what was best for me and my children first. I know that as parents we must appear like we have everything under control and give our children stability.

There were times when I just had to pray and ask God to truly help me to raise my children, because I had a lot to learn and did not always feel prepared. When I chose to have a child very early in my life, I did not realize that I also put myself in a position to have very little personal time or space for what I needed. I was always focused on making sure my children had everything that they needed. It took some time for me to really grasp that, as much as they needed me, I needed me even more. All I wanted was for them to know that I was there for them and their desires, purposes, and goals. As a mom, I knew that I had to protect my children, which was very easy for me to do when they were smaller. As they started to get older, I had to pray more and advise less. I was not that good with allowing them to experience things on their own. I wanted to be right there when things did not work out. I did not want them to feel any type of disappointment, because I knew that they dealt with a lot after their dad left us. I realized I was overcompensating, trying my best to make sure they did not have any other pressures in life. What a big mistake that was for me. My children all dealt with my separation from their father in different ways. They never gave me a hard time because they knew I was doing all I could do for them, however, they internalized everything, and, as they got older, it started to surface in a way that was very unhealthy for them. I noticed that all of them experienced lack of self-worth in different ways. I know they all are individuals, but as a mom, I could see the same pattern in each of them. It is very hurtful to witness your child(ren) going through life with a lot of emotional trauma and not being able to help physically. I would pray about it and let it be something between them and God to handle. It really shows how powerless we are and how much we need God to help us support someone in prayer. For one of my children, transitioning from one thing to another was very difficult to do. It is amazing how people function and sometimes you have to really find out why we operate the way we do. It took several episodes before my child realized that they needed support from others to help them to identify and discover some things for themselves. Life is not as easy as we think sometimes.

I wish I would have better prepared my children with real life experiences. I know for me it was easier to do things for my children, than teaching them to do it for themselves. Sometimes we depend on others to do what we need to do for our own children. Once I realized those things, I started changing for my next child. I know that most older children feel like they had it hard and when they see how a parent raises their siblings it appears that some were favored, and others were not. I would like to shed some light on that mindset. For me, it was not favoritism, instead it was the fact that I was maturing and starting to really know how to handle situations better. When it came to my next child, I knew how to address things better. I know that life is full of problems, so it is important for me to have a more solution-based approach with my children. Together we could figure out an effective plan that would rescue them in their situation. I do understand that we may not be able to fix everything, but at least I could say that I tried. It is important to know that learning is a part of the process and figuring things out is what matters when we are facing problems in life. I know problems exist, but I want to make sure a plan is set in place after the problem has been identified. I know that with my children's generation, they want things instantly and never want to sit back and wait. That is why so many of them think that drugs, sex, and so many unhealthy resources are the answer. The answer is really learning how to love yourself, living in joy and peace, and learning how to be patient for things. I encourage them to "start your day with a happy vibe and when life appears you know how to redirect yourself back to that place". LWB Butterfly.

As a seasoned adult, I have truly soul-searched things I have learned as a mom and things that I can do better. If you talk with my children, I know they will say I did great raising them, but I know that there is always room for improvement. As my children continue to grow, I will always be a listening ear for them. Therefore, I am channeling my mind on my personal growth more now. I remember something that my dad told me. He said, "Lisa, there is no tomorrow". I said, "What do you mean daddy?" and he said, "when the next day comes, it is called "today", so do not put off for tomorrow, because it will never show up". At that time, I did not know what he meant by that, but now I do. Tomorrow is not a guarantee for anyone, therefore we must grasp the fact that living in the present moment is what we need and not allowing our emotions to make us feel like we are not accomplishing our daily and weekly goals.

It is time to stop feeling like a failure when things happen. That was hard, because when my marriage ended, I felt like a failure and it caused me to never get back into another relationship. I know that was a bit to the extreme, but I had that mindset for several years. That divorce really affected me, reason being we both dedicated our lives to God and I never thought infidelity nor divorce would ever be a part of my story. That was a tremendous challenge that I had to face as an adult. I had to deal with it daily and at one point it really consumed my being. I had to come up with a master plan that would help me activate my inner being and then learn how to operate in it rather than staying dormant. It took a while for me, but I finally started looking at my challenge as a blessing.

I learned how to face my challenges and see things through my Creator's lens. He was teaching me how to handle my situations wisely and maturely. I was finally starting to explore alternative views about my new life journey and discover how to improve myself for my own good. It is amazing how situations can take you out of your true character. My situation caused me to become very irritable and it changed my view of life and God. For a while, I was mad at God, because I felt like I did what he asked of me and yet what I desired the most was destroyed. I had to learn that God was helping me to find myself, because He knew that I had consumed myself with my ex-husband and our children. He was showing me who I really was by introducing me to myself. It was a great discovery and amazing. I was learning to be willing to reach out for help and started receiving advice and opinions from others in a positive and respectful way. Some things that I was hearing was hurtful, but the bible says the truth sets you free. It did not say it would not hurt. I was seeking support from those who I knew had my best interest at heart without feeling embarrassed, intimidated, nor threatened by their views. When I shared my thoughts with others I had to make sure I was optimistic and not pessimistic. There were times when I did not agree with what was shared with me, but I still was not rude with those who were pouring into my life. Some of their ideas were right on point and they were not too far off from my own ideas. I know those who were helping me were spirit-led people, therefore, I know they were seeking God's wisdom as they were help-ing me. I had to know that my way of thinking could have been tarnished and that my way was not *the* way. I really wanted to do things God's way with everything I was experiencing in my life. My life was so closed in, it was like I was living in a box. I had to learn how to be more diverse because God is not a close- minded being. This world offers so many good things and I had to discover them for myself. As an adult we think that once we reach a certain age we cannot pursue our dreams, especially if it was not accomplished by a certain time in our life. I had to learn how to make the universe a more beautiful place and tap into a new mindset. When I was seek-ing advice from people, I knew that I was not going to agree with everything, but it was good to hear and see from another prospective. If I did not agree, I simply just appreciated what they were trying to de-liver to me. It was important for me not to be a controller of others. I knew that I had to only control myself. That is why I love the serenity prayer so much. It placed everything in order for me. I did not want to control what someone else had observed of me and my situation. I was experiencing how to have a yielding spirit.

When we get a job, we often strive to do everything perfectly and that could add on pressure. That is the same for life issues. I had to realize that nothing and nobody was perfect. We are human and we will make mistakes. Things will get messed up and not work out sometimes. My pliability was off track just a bit. I was operating mostly off a fantasy as it related to life, because when setbacks happened, it really took me a long time to redirect myself. I had to learn how to have a strong comeback when I got knocked down. Have you ever talked with someone and they tell you that when things go wrong it is the enemy attacking you? I disagree. I know that the enemy cannot do anything to me without my permission. Once I got that truth it made things easier for me to accept. In life everything that does not work out for us is not from the devil. I had to train myself not to get so easily disappointed and have feelings of being rejected when things just do not go my way. I had to grow up and at this point of being a seasoned adult I had to do better because I knew better. I love Maya Angelou's quote that told us, "Do the best you can until you know better. Then when you know better, do better." I was willing to focus on my rejections and disappointments, but not to the point of it keeping me from moving forward and going where God was leading me.

The hardest part of dealing with life during a storm is staying calm and making sure my deportment was good. One thing that helped me was I had to study Galatians 5:22 because this message was my only way to live life with all the attributes that God had given to me as a person. I had to dig deep to understand that I could not move forward without having inner peace. Now I have always heard about the fruit of the spirit, but I had to learn how to really eat from those fruits. One thing I discovered was I could not operate in it without surrendering my spirit and soul to God. I really had to process the fact that those fruits could not be produced by me. I had to understand that if I wanted love, I had to know what love looks like to God. If I wanted peace, I had to seek God for it. I simply had to learn how to operate in the fruit of the spirit with the mindset of my Creator. I could not have any of those fruits without Him. I was trying to do it without Him and I kept finding myself back in the same emotional pattern every time. The only way I was going to survive that storm after my divorce was if I calmed down by yielding to God's ultimate peace. I knew I would have days that felt like my peace would never return and when that happened I went into my secret place and surrendered to God's presence. When I entered I felt alone, but when I departed I knew that everything was going to be ok. I remember going through something with one of my children and I just knew that the only way we would be set free is if we put all our problems, emotions, and thoughts in His hands. When the storm is so strong, I had to learn how to stop and say, "Lisa, God has you and your cares because you gave them to Him, so chill out and watch the work of the Lord." Trust me when I say, I have witnessed His power when I stop talking and kneel down in prayer. Feeling calm all the time is not a reality, however, my goal is to always try to have it. As an adult we may not have our earthly parents to guide us. We have to learn how to tap into our spiritual being and allow our Creator to protect us, support us, and lead us in the right direction. At this point is when I was living out my most genuine confidence in Him. I was cleansed and purged from who I was, and I started committing to God. I was not feeling victimized nor bamboozled by my situation anymore. I was not allowing my triumph to be a determining factor anymore. I was in this storm of being a single mom, and I was going to endure it with all of God's wisdom and power. I could not let challenges stop the opportunities that I was about to explore. I had to become assessable to God and understand that my broken heart was being repaired by Him. I know people think we are special when we talk to ourselves, but that is something I did quite frequently. I would ask myself some tough yet needed questions.

Not only did I need to be assessable to God, I needed to be that with people as well. I had to learn how to trust again and I wanted to make sure I was approachable with everyone. I realized I was taking my life issues out on others and I had to stop doing that because I was beginning to feel like I was not approachable. I could not allow one person and situation to shape my entire being anymore. I needed to become transparent with others and not be so defensive. I was learning to converse with others without having a melt-down. I was learning to be stronger and control my emotions. One way for me to do that was to encourage and appreciate myself. Instead of me waiting for others to praise or compliment me, I learned how to do that for myself. I was releasing the shame and embracing the good feeling of making things happen for myself as an individual and being proud of myself for trying. I was not looking for approval from my ex anymore. Honestly, I was beginning not to even care what he thought of me anymore. I was more concerned with what I thought of my own actions. I was growing up. I was feeling free.

Now is that something that the enemy really wanted me to do for myself? No, it was not! I realized that God was working for my good the entire time. God was teaching me how to be confident in who I am and erase all the lies I had heard about myself from my ex. Now, I know he was entitled to think what he wanted of me. I was just not receiving nor processing it anymore. His views of me were very pessimistic and I realized that I should stop listening to anything that was coming out of his mouth. For one, I was not allowing his opinions to determine who I was as a woman. I know who I am and to whom I belong. I was learning to trust myself and the choices I was making. I was not looking for approval from someone who had abandoned me and our children anymore. I was letting go of all the absurdities that I was engulfed in when I was with him.

It was time for me to start living my adult life with pride and start to have fun in life. I was so rigid, and I needed to loosen up a bit. I had to work hard at not taking everything that I did so seriously. Yes, life is serious, but it is also a fun journey as well. Loosening up did not mean not being responsible, it simply meant that I was more than a mom! I had to know I have only one life and I was going to leave it with no regrets. It was time for me to laugh with others and just have fun. If God said that laughter is good for my soul, then it was time for me to do just that. I am not much of a comedian, but I said to myself that I would tell jokes every now and then just because it makes me feel good. Just because we are adults does not mean we have to be to the extreme about every-thing. It is time to live and not just exist. It means we are fully aware of our emotions and we can face difficulties in a healthy way. I do not have to make decisions based on my emotions, instead I have learned how to make decisions in a more mature and self-assured type of way. As adults we do have to take control over of our lives, and not forget to get God's directions. He has given us a mind to have our own dreams and His promises can motivate us to success and be great role models for the next gener-ation. During this stage, we should concentrate on our visions and goals so we can experience a creative joyful, healthy, and well-rounded life-style. It is a time where we can be respectful toward ourselves and others in a mature way. This will help us live a more peaceful life. This process may take some time because it is new for you, so do not give up on want-ing to live a new way. Be determined to operate with a strong mindset that is full of positive energy, pro-vision, and courage. I am suggesting that you not be so hard on yourself and take one day at a time, one project at a time, and never stop praying for yourself and others. During this adult stage we must remember to surrender ourselves to God and ask Him to keep working with and on us!

MASTERMIND

1. What does adulthood mean to you?

2. How can you clean up your mindset as it relates to being an adult?

3. Do you feel the need to make any changes in your adulthood?

4. What is the sorbet (refresher) you would like to see happen in your life? What are some palates (life choices) would you desire to change?

FINISH THESE SENTENCES:

1. As an adult I will ___________________

   ______________________________________.

2. It is time for me to start _________________

   _______________________________________.

3. Being an adult does not mean ____________

   _______________________________________.

SCRIPTURES M-P:

M – My son, give me thine heart. – Proverbs 23:26

N – No man can serve two masters. – Matthew 6:24

O – O give thanks unto the Lord; for He is good. – Psalm 118:1

P – Praise ye the Lord: for it is good to sing praises unto our God. – Psalm 147:1

CHAPTER FIVE

FISH

"It is time to give and to receive"

CAREER

Fish is a very popular entrée, filled with high quality nutrients including the vitamin D that we need in our body without having to take extra supplements. Fish is also known for enriching our mind by providing omega-3 fatty acids. It provides several benefits for us such as: reducing diseases like heart attacks and strokes, just by eating it a few times a week. It is essential for human body development such as our eyes and it helps with our memory. This food type helps with depression and improves the overall autoimmune diseases that can form in our bodies. It lowers the possibilities of developing asthma and it improves our sleep habits.

During the career stage of life, adults begin making choices that will strengthen their skills and allow them to function in whatever activity/position that they desire. If we explore the benefits of this phase of life, our choices can be well thought out and balanced for a better outcome in our life. When we make decisions for our future it is important to consider the fact that we are choosing to do something that creates financial stability and happiness. If we do things out of obligation rather than choice, we could find ourselves dealing with things such as health issues that could have been avoided if we took the time to make sure that what we are working toward what truly works for us. When I started to make career choices, it was just to make some money for my son and myself. Later in life I realized that I had to do something that I was passionate about because it made me feel better about myself and I was more motivated to deal with difficult situations because I was willing to learn how to handle it without walking away.

When you invest in something it is not so easy to walk away from it. I remember that my dream was to always be a teacher, but life happened, and I did not see a way to make that a part of my life once I had started my family. Sometimes we can delay our own dreams because of doubt. Yes, I did have some detours, but they were not dead-ends. Eventually, I became a teacher and will share my journey with you in hopes that my advice can help you to pursue your dream as well. My dream did become my reality and I love it.

As a young adult with a child, I knew that I had to provide for my son. I worked at a grocery store and clothing store while I was finishing up high school, but I wanted more for myself. I just did not know how to do it. I knew that I was not going to college, because I wanted to take care of my son and see him develop as much as I could. I remember one day talking with my auntie and she told me about a job opportunity at a well-known university. So, I applied and guess what, I got it. I was so excited! I had benefits for my son and myself and I felt so proud of myself. I even had the opportunity to work with my aunt. We shared so many moments that I will never forget. That experience was more than a job for me. While I was there I learned so much about life, diversity, and understanding the differences in people without being intimidated by it.

One thing that excited me about working at a university was experiencing part of the campus lifestyle. Even though I was not a student myself, I supported students and their needs. It was good to see how college life worked, because I did not go there after my high school education. Nevertheless, God still allowed me to see what it was like because He knew my heart's desire. I was surrounded by so many educators, professors, and leaders. God had a plan for me and I did not even know it. That is how He handles me because He knows I need baby steps when entering into new things. It was nice being able to go to work in an environment where I was surrounded by educated people.

I had worked on campus for over 16 years before God opened the door for me to become a teacher. He knew that I needed some experience with the culture of education first. I had to be molded because I was so clueless about the schooling process. My first job was in the housing department and I was responsible for placing students in the residential halls and keeping up with their repairs, keys, and issues that were found in their rooms. I eventually became a supervisor for over 25 student workers. Then I applied for a position in the financial aid office, and there I was responsible for entering in loan amounts and learning the process of filing student loan information. Next, I relocated to the career and planning department where I had to help students place themselves in a career that they were interested in. I had to help them set goals for themselves and then help them to identify their job choices such as: social work, investigator, creative, and entrepreneurial jobs. That was interesting because once the students saw the breakdown they knew that making those decisions would place them on a path toward future opportunities. When it was time to discuss the salary part of a career, that really gave them a reality check of realizing that they were either picking that career because they really loved it or because it was based on the amount of money that they would be earning.

As an educator now, I realize that my choice was based on my love for children. My next job on campus was when I worked in the chancellor's office. That experience was more reserved than any other department that I was accustomed to. It was all about getting the work done in the most accurate and professional manner possible. The energy was esoteric, therefore, working there was toilsome at times. I made the best of it because I knew that having this combination of work would be necessary for my resume. My final campus experience was in the fleet service department. I was able to see how student transportation was handled as they had to travel throughout the campus. It was interesting discovering the details of the car rental process and ordering gas for the pumps at the campus station.

All my involvement on campus prepared me for my transition from the corporate world into the educational world. My evolution was not even planned. While working at the university, I became pregnant with my last baby and I went on maternity leave from work. I did not know that at that point in life I was not ever going back to the university again. My time was up. I just did not know what my next step was going to be. While I was on leave, I did part-time work with one of my dearest friends. She asked me if I would be interested in working for her and her husband in their company. I was flattered by her request, but I had no property management skills. They believed enough in me and hired me. I ended up loving the job and really it was a place of refuge for me. I was in the mist of dealing with a very unhealthy marriage, a small baby, and two other young children.

God knew I needed their presence to get me through that tough, emotional, and unstable time in my life. I was in a failing marriage and I knew it. There were so many hurtful things that I was dealing with. My husband who I thought was my soul mate ended up not being that person. He wanted out of the marriage because he wanted his freedom. It was so hard to process that as my reality. I was not a wife anymore. I did not know what in the world I was going to do nor how I was going to do it. I had small children, and I felt so alone and abandoned. So, this job was a true outlet for me. I remember going to my friend one day and just broke down with her. I was damaged and felt like there was no recovery for me. I was in such a bad state of mind that I really did not care too much about my appearance. So, when I arrived at her doorstep she looked at me and said, "Whose wig is that and why do you have a hole in your pants?" All I could do was laugh and cry because I knew I looked a mess! The type of friendship we share is inseparable and I knew she was coming from a good place, because she had never seen me look like that before. I told her that it was my mom's wig and at that point we both laughed. She invited me to come into her house and she just let me do what I needed to do, which was to simply cry all my pain away. She did not even attempt to stop me, and it was so therapeutic. I shared all my true feelings of embarrassment with her and she just listened to me. Sometimes that is all you need from a friend. This helped me to get myself together. I had to come up with a plan for myself and the first way for me to do that was to cleanse myself from low self-esteem.

I picked myself back up and started appearing like the person I once was. Working at the job with my friend was so helpful, because we were together every day and that is exactly what I needed. They even allowed me to bring my baby to work so that I could save some money and not pay daycare. As I reflect on that, I was so blessed to have people like them in my life. I was helping them with their business and they were helping me with my life. I was starting to think positively again, I was feeling my heart beat again. I was living again, and it was a good feeling. I was surrounded by optimistic energy and I loved it. Their company is established on faith and at that time in my life, that is all I truly had to rely on. Remember, I was on maternity leave when this job opportunity came to me, and it was time for me to go back to work at the university, but my time was up. One day the CEO of the company told me he wanted to meet with me and during the meeting he told me he would match my salary if I would stay with his company. I could not believe it and as much as I wanted to say yes right then and there, I told him that I would pray about it and let him know something in a few days. It was at that moment I knew I had to make a very tough but necessary decision. I was struggling with ending my comfort zone of working with the state because it truly was a great opportunity, however, I knew I was at the end of my road there. So, I did what my spirit lead me to do and I accepted the position on a full-time basis.

Now, that was big for me because I was taking a risk. I never made decisions without getting others' advice. For the first time, I made a choice with only me and God. It was awesome, and I felt good about it. Now I know why I had to be there. That is where my true discovery of my career began to happen. One day while I was at work a man came into the office and asked if he could leave some brochures with us regarding enrollment at a college in the area. At that time my friend looked at me and said, "You know this is for you right?" I asked her, "What in the world are you talking about?" She said, "You know you have always wanted to get your degree." I told her she was absolutely right.

I enrolled at the college seeking my business degree. I went through the same process that I helped students with when I worked at the university, so it made sense to me and I was not afraid of anything, because I knew what I was doing. God had already given me the experience; therefore, I was not intimidated by anything. The program was for adults, so I did not have to feel bad about seeking my degree at the age of 36. I could not believe that I was going to college. I did not let the fact that I had three small children stop me. I was acting out on faith and it felt good. I was a student! It was unbelievable for me. I was not going to look at this opportunity as being hard for me. I wanted to enjoy every moment, class, and experience. I took 18 hours each semester, not because I was rushing, but because I was loving it. It was very intense, but I was not going to allow stress nor bad energy to interrupt what was so exciting for me. I made the dean's list every semester and I graduated in three years versus four years. During my senior year I felt a shift in my spirit and did not know why. I was heard the voice of God speaking to me and reminding me of my childhood desire to teach. I was like "God, I am ok. I am at the end of a business degree. I will be fine." He said "Lisa, this is your time, go get it"!

I started looking into a master's program for elementary education. Right after I graduated from undergrad, I immediately enrolled at a university that allowed me to pursue a master's in education even though my undergraduate degree was in business. Now during this time, I had no experience in education and God allowed me an opportunity to work at a local charter school as a teacher's assistant to get a feel of how a teacher functions. I was surrounded by educators all my life and to work with them was unbelievable. I was like a sponge, I wanted to know all about the educational world. I got involved in different committees at the school and went to a lot of professional developmental (PD) workshops. The bible says, "My people perish because of lack of knowledge" (Hosea 4:6). I did not want that for myself. During my course load I learned so much and having the hands-on classroom experience was the best thing for me. I met two awesome teachers and to this day they are still my mentors. They took time and shared information with me. They were patient with me and I will forever love and admire their professionalism. It took years of experience before I could understand the purpose of teaching. It is not just being in front of students and having power over them. It is building relationships with parents, students, and the community.

My mentors are still in education; however, they are seeking administrative roles now. We need people like them surrounding our children every single day. As you know, being a teacher requires earning your certification with the state. I am in the process of earning that highly qualified ranking. The test is very challenging, but I am not defeated. I will earn it and I know it does not define who I am as an educator. It only qualifies me to show others that I have completed the entire process to become a teacher within the state. I have to say that I did not always view it from this perspective, because I have taken the test and did not pass it. (Then the state changed the test in the midst of me studying for it and that did not help, because I had to change my study materials. Truthfully, I was afraid to face this challenge, because it reminded me of my experience in school as a child.) For a moment I allowed the little girl in me to give up because I was not going to be qualified enough to earn my certificate. I had to talk her down and remove her from my thought process. Once I did, the fear faded, and I had to find a way to help myself out.

I have a great support team. My sister would always tell me that I am a teacher with or without a piece of paper. I really appreciated that, but I still knew what I would feel when I received it. I knew that I could not hold myself up from being a blessing to children and their education. My first teaching experience started with my own children and mainly my baby. At this point in my life I knew I wanted to be involved in his educational journey. So, I made sure I knew what was going on so that I could fully equip him. Just like anything else in life, changes will happen and now education is more data driven than anything else. I had to learn all the ins and outs of education so that my son would not struggle in school like I did.

As you know, teachers are off from work in the summer months, and I was not used to that. I had to come up with a plan that would allow my children and I to function during those 10 weeks. My first year in a school I was asked to work the summer camp and that was great, however, the next year I was not asked to serve in the school during the summer. So, one day I was sharing with a friend of the idea of opening a summer enrichment program. I knew it was not going to be easy, but I had my business experience to help guide me, and I started my own summer camp enrichment program that continues to grow each year. This journey has kept me connected to my dream of teaching because it helps me to prepare students for their next school year and to make sure they do not have any summer loss problems when they return to school. I know what it is like to struggle in school, especially with reading. I have learned that the school system is not designed to really help low-level learning students so that is why I pour my heart into what I do because I know they do not get support like they should in school. I am not saying this to bash anyone or any system, however, I am saying it from the perspective of the needs of low-level learners. I teach using strategies that are tailored to support struggling students. I have a true love for learning and teaching. When I was in school I only remember one teacher really taking extra time out to help me and to this day that means so much to me. As a student I was overlooked a lot because I was very quiet and never gave teachers any problems. I did not like trouble. One may think that that was a good thing, but really it wasn't because most of my teachers paid no attention to me. They only focused on two types of students: those who made excellent grades and those who had behavioral issues.

When God reminded me of my desire to teach, so much stirred back up in me that I forgot about. One thing that triggered me to move forward in this case was to help be a part of students' growth and to make sure that they did not have any struggles with who they were and how they learned. Now, you may be a person who is seeking guidance on how to make your career choice and I want to share several steps toward identifying your ideal career. Please understand that age is not a factor. I was 36 years old before I even earned my undergraduate degree in business and then enrolled into a master's program for education because my undergrad degree was in business. Prior to that, I did not even think about having a career in education anymore, because I thought my time was up. Then I realized that as long as I was alive, my dream was too. I have discovered the beauty of teaching and do not have to brainstorm anymore. If you are still in the brainstorming stage with your career think about what you are passionate about. "Find it, Love it, and Live it" -LWB Butterfly.

It is time to find out what inspires you to the point that you just want to make it known to others. I realize now that I am important enough to accomplish what I want for my life so that I will always be a goal seeker and not just a dreamer. I knew that for me to become an educator I had to prepare myself and attend a program in school that would educate me in the areas I needed to become an effective teacher. You may not have to go to school, but it may help for you to get some experience in the industry you are interested in. I am so glad that I had an opportunity to work and volunteer in education, because it helped me to be confident in my choice. I knew that I was pursuing the right field for myself. I decided to leave a state job of over 16 years in order to understand the world of education and I am happy I made that change for myself. It was a sacrifice, but it was truly necessary for me to have done that. I know that I would never have understood education if I did not get the proper training and guidance that I received when I left my corporate job. When I started working in my career, I felt more settled within myself. I was not just working for a check. I was really doing something that was reflecting my heart and skill set.

A career is another way to identify who you are in life and what you can offer to society. Having an occupation may require a lot of your time and sometimes it can take you from your family, and other obligations because you become so passionate in what you are doing, but it is important to have a well-balance approach so that you do not launch into something that is going to cause a negative energy toward something that you enjoy doing. It may take up a significant amount of your life, because of the opportunities you will need for progress. Just have a strong and effective solution that will help you manage your time and get back in a positive head space with yourself and possibly your family. Sometimes your profession can interrupt your entire life, so it is important to be very mindful not to allow that to happen.

I know personally, that was one of the reasons that my relationship had ended. He did not know how to juggle a family and his career at the same time. His priorities were out of order; therefore, he became married to his career and our family suffered from it. It will happen so quickly that you will not even see it coming. One day you look up and your life is in shambles all because you are too busy doing what you love and forgot how to nurture everything else. I was very happy for him finally doing what he loved, but he loved it so much that he lost focus of everything and everyone else.

Being in a career can be demanding and I know that. I must make sure that I do put my family first. I know that without the money we cannot provide, but having the money with no family is no better. I really am speaking to people who have a family, because when you are single, there are no boundaries to really set nor follow. However, if you are going to consider being in a relationship please think about these possible adjustments. I also want to add that just because a person may be single does not mean that they will not have to deal with balancing their career with themselves. What I mean by that is a single person can be so consumed with their work that they forget to take care of themselves physically, mentally, socially, and spiritually.

Within family, it can be very hard to choose between your personal and professional lifestyles and if your partner/family knows what your expectations are it should help your situation much better. I remember working so hard for my children that I forgot to spend quality time with them for a while and then my spirit helped me to get back on track. My baby son is a basketball player and I was planning for him to get to practice because I was tutoring. I was upset when I found out he had to wait for someone or ride home with someone else most of the time. I had to adjust my schedule and start attending his practices just so that he could see my face and know that I care and was there for him. (You should have seen how he was showing out for his mommy.) At that moment I knew that I had to continue to balance my life out to be there for him. I felt bad for the times that I was not there, but I learned to stop punishing myself for my past mistakes. I also had to do that for my children's father. My middle son and I have long talks sometimes and one day he shared something with me that just set my soul free. We were talking about his father and some of the choices that he made with this family, and he told me that he truly has forgiven his dad for leaving us. I asked him what made him feel that way and he told me that no one has ever truly exonerated his dad for being a human and parent. He said that he still had good qualities even with the "bad" choices that he made. This made me realize just how much I did not forgive my children's father for his choices once we had ended our relationship. I know this is a start to a new beginning for me.

We all want to be successful in our profession, however, it is just as important to be successful in our personal lives as well. We acquire a career because we have some energy inside us that is creative and want to share it with the world. Our career desires really start when we are children. Children dream about what they want to be when they grow up. It is fine to dream, however, we need to set goals as well. My dream of being a teacher was planted when I was a little girl, but it did not appear like it would ever happen for me because of the path that I had taken earlier in my young adult life. Even though I was working in the corporate world, my teaching experience was established even then in a different way. I was not physically in the classroom; however, I was still placed in an educational environment by being at the university. I know that teaching is my career, but we are such multifaceted people that we do not have to limit ourselves to just one career. I was able to combine my business and educational experience and see them compliment who I am. I did not have to choose one over the other. I used my skills with both opportunities and they did not overlap one another. Now I know that just because I had a job in business that did not make it a career choice. I have worked with computers and performed administrative duties that helped me in education.

The essence of a career is to seek after your purpose in life to serve our society. I was called to teach and was able to intertwine business into my career.

Both worked out together for my good and did not cause me to be limited in achieving what I wanted to do in life. My career allows me to serve young people and to help them to improve their lives. That is a masterpiece all in one for me. The amalgamation of teaching and business has empowered me to continue to love my career. Having an occupation requires the necessary time and attention but remember to try not to dismiss other important responsibilities that you are obligated to. Your career path should not put you in a box, instead it should liberate you to live out your dreams and goals. Now that I have been working in my career five years, I still have long and short-term goals. I think it is very healthy for everyone to set goals just because it caused me to determine my ultimate objectives in my career.

I want to share something with you that is very dear to me and was very scary to deal with. One of my loved ones was diagnosed with having a mental condition during the ages of 18 -23. They are a very loving and caring person who was dealing with so much of life that they just could not handle it anymore. Their profession was one of a physical intensity and they enjoyed it so much so that it caused a mental meltdown. Watching this happen to someone I care about was about the hardest thing for me to face. I had to see them react in ways that was totally out of their character and there was nothing I could do about it. All I could do was trust God for a spiritual breakthrough. They did not share all their feelings regarding the pressures of their career until they hit rock bottom. They loved it so much that they did not even realize how stressful it was on their body and life. They did not want to face the thought of not performing on stage again. It took several episodes until they were able to face the fact that their career could have possibly caused their medical condition. They have support from so many people and now they are on the road to a permanent healthier place. One of the struggles was having to take medication to help them to function and have a better way of looking at things. They are very conscious of what goes in their body for physical reasons, but they were unaware they needed that same mindset with their mental state as well. Their desire was to take holistic medicine, however, in our society researchers have not found those types of herbs to be as effective as the supplements that have to be FDA approved. He went to counseling for help and became willing to take the medication. He is now adjusting to life in a more sensible manner.

I am sharing this because I want you to understand that having a career is a good and bad venture if you are not able to handle the pressures that come with the job. There are some positions that come with a lot of pressure and you have to be willing to face the facts and deal with them. It may be a possibility that you cannot emotionally, physically, nor mentally handle. I do not want anyone to experience what my loved one and I had to face. Please be mindful that life does offer us an opportunity to have a career, but we cannot allow it to have us. So, if you are dealing with the any emotional stress as it relates to your career, please seek help so that you can understand how to adjust your mindset and life to accommodate your love for what you want to do on this earth. Do not allow it to take control of you; take a stand and make decisions that will be beneficial for you and your life's journey. Identify your position and make it an achievable goal that will truly cause you to have a well-balanced personal and professional networking system. If you have not sat down with yourself and really processed what you want, please take time out and do it. No matter what life brings, you are the only one who can embrace or dismiss opportunities for yourself. I had to make long and short-term goals in education that helped me to focus on my ultimate career objectives, rather than moving purposelessly from job to job. I am finally on a strong, interchangeable, and adventurous journey. I am finally happy with myself. When I go to work every day, I really feel good about it. I don't just do this to provide for my family, it is more meaningful to me than that. My career is important to me just like my relationship with God is. I must serve Him because I enjoy it and I know that it is the best thing for me. I worship Him because I enjoy the connection that I have with Him. I study His word because it keeps me rooted in doing things that are right toward Him, myself, and others.

When we understand why we make choices, we have a clearer purpose for our lives. Every day I commit to happiness, which comes from within. When our choices are in line with our heart's desires, we experience happiness. Believe in what you want. Find it, Love it, and Live it! It will require sacrificing sometimes, but it is worth it if you are truly ready for it. Just do not let the sacrifice be your life. If no one supports you, it is okay. You should not be seeking others' approval of your life anyway. Be wise and make yourself happy. When it is time for you to interview, know that your potential employer has already read up on your abilities. Go in with confidence and remove any insecurities after you have done your own research and you know what you truly want. It does not matter when it happens, just as long as it happens. Time is not a factor for your dreams. When I invited God into my life I had some doubts, but I knew that based on what I learned about Him I had made the right decision. I had to make sure I understood what I committed myself to and dedicate myself to God and His promises for my life.

My career was no different; I knew I had to keep my goals fresh. Make sure you have an efficacious strategy to reach your spiritual and professional goals and keep yourself on the right track. Setting goals is very important and if you do not set them it may cause you to have a delay in your plans or possibly not be able to complete them. As you know, life will happen and that can cause some delays, but try your best not to purposely delay them because you did not create goals for yourself. Try not to allow anything to override your professional objectives. Make sure you pray about it and get the best guidance possible so that you will feel comfortable and have clarity on your new career journey. If you face a door being closed, try not to force it back open. It could possibly be God removing you from a situation that you cannot handle. Try not to question your capabilities if the position you wanted fell through. Just say, "What God has for me is for me" and then trust God for His plan for your life. When your door does open, and you are mastering your duties, find something that can challenge you in another area. Do not ever give up on what you want, just be willing to accept that if God has something else for you, walk in it with a willing and peaceful mindset. It is time to give and to receive. Remember, "Life requires you to serve and be served" - LWB Butterfly.

MASTERMIND

1. Are you happy where you are in your career at this point? Explain.

2. Are you actively involved in doing things that you are passionate about?

3. What's preventing you from engaging in activities or careers that you want?

4. Is your career too much for you and are you willing to find something else?

FINISH THESE SENTENCES:

1. I realize I am happy in my career because _____

    _____________________________________.

2. I will keep my passion by __________________

    ___________________________________.

3. I will not prevent myself from ______________

    ___________________________________.

SCRIPTURES Q – T:

Q – Quit you like men, be strong. – 1 Corinthians 16:13

R – Remember the sabbath day, to keep it holy. – Exodus 20:8

S – Seek ye the Lord while He may be found, call upon Him while He is near. – Isaiah 55:6

T – Thou God seest me. – Genesis 16:13

CHAPTER SIX

MAIN COURSE

*"Draw near to God and He will
draw near to you"*

Salvation-Many Members One Body

This dish is the primary meal and can include many different combinations of food. It usually includes a meat, which has a high level of protein that strengthens the body and builds muscles. This meal may include carbohydrates that consist of glucose and provide energy. Vegetables are also usually included in this meal. During the main course of life, adults discover the importance of having a relationship with God and learn how they can strengthen their faith. Just like protein, carbohydrates, and vegetables all serve a purpose for providing our body with what it needs, we need salvation and a relationship with God to keep us connected and grow to the highest level we can in God. This relationship allows us to gain power, faith, and endurance that we cannot achieve alone. We know that there are many features in the main course and all of them have a purpose for our body. As believers we need each other the same way. There are many members in one body and we all have a purpose for serving God and each other. "True living is when you allow your inner man to appear outwardly" LWB Butterfly.

Life is meant to change and if you refuse to accept that, you may not be able to move forward mentally nor spiritually. I love butterflies and one reason is because I love their lifecycle. A butterfly starts as a caterpillar and then during the growth process it forms into a pupa and then a chrysalis covers it for safety. During that process a butterfly is formed. The wings are weak in the beginning, but in time they gain strength and the butterfly begins to fly. When I really think about this I get so excited about life. We all start out in life in the form of an egg. As time passes we become what our Creator intended for us to be for His glory. I know we hear this a lot, but it is a true statement. We must trust God enough with our life to live under His subjection. We are two-part beings, human and spirit. At a young age I started allowing my spirit to counsel me and send me information that would prepare me for things to come. God's Holy Spirit was in me and He cultivated me to follow His plan and multiply what He gave me. For example, God provides us with strawberries, and the creativity in us causes us to want more from it, so we use that berry to create jam, cakes, and pies. The provision is the strawberry, and the multiplication comes from us.

We are so creative that sometimes we can become overwhelmed and our creativity can be blocked. This will happen when you are overloaded with too many things. Creative people tend to have so many things going on in our minds that we can drop the ball on all of them if we are not mindful. We must allow our spirits to balance us so that we can be successful without pressure and achieve the goals that we are setting for ourselves.

I want to share a few things about my experience with salvation that truly blessed me to the point that I wanted to surrender myself to God for the rest of my life. There is a picture titled "Footprints" that shows the image of Jesus and a man walking. As they continue to walk there is only one-foot print been shown, because Jesus was carrying the man the rest of way. In life we must know that God is with us and we are never alone. I had to learn that when I was facing the lowest points in my life that God was there. I was taught that God would never leave nor forsake me and I had to believe that when life was showing me something else. I felt comfort knowing that when things were happening in my life God already knew about it and was teaching me how to handle it. We all deal with things, but there comes a point when we must really know that God has us. I had to learn how not to dwell on my problems and learn to pray about them and let it go. I was learning how to deal with things in my life the way God would. We all have learned behavior from our childhood, and if the influence was not good then we find ourselves doing things inappropriately. We are human and will make mistakes, but we must allow our spirits to be redeemed so that we can live. We must stop being broken vessels. "Do not allow life to make you so easily broken that you are hard to repair" - LWB Butterfly.

I used to think that my marriage was my life, therefore, I could not identify anything else that I was doing. I had to mature in God so that He could help me to understand my life was more than being in a relationship. I had so much in me and was surprised when I started exploring my abilities. When I started to use my gifts, it was an amazing feeling. God was confirming what He was telling me to do. I had to know He was real and that His words over me were true. I could not guess or believe, because those feelings were a possibility. I needed to know in my soul that what God was saying was truth for me to follow. That is why your salvation is so important. It is not for anyone else to understand, it is personal. Connecting with God is the best relationship that we could ever have because it causes us to dig deep inside and become all that our creator wants us to be.

I was talking with a sweet lady one day and she told me her brother was very sick and may not make it. I know that sounds bad and for a moment I was sad about that news. What lifted my spirits was what she said afterward. She said that her brother gave his life to God and was the happiest that he had ever been in his life. He said, "if God wants to come for me He can," and shortly after that he passed away. I know that we all look for things and even people to make us happy, but there is truly nothing like serving God and living the way He wants you to live. When I committed to God, I felt good in my mind, body, and soul. It can be hard to explain this to people who have not experienced it, so it is important to be great examples for people because we are representing God. I have come across a lot of people who confess their salvation, but they are so judgmental with people and how they live their life. It is not up to us to draw someone to Christ, however, showing a spirit of kindness is the magnet for them to connect to. I discovered the truth that God is merciful while people (Christian/spiritual or not) are indeed judgmental. Now that was very confusing for me because those judgmental people were the ones preaching hard about God and His expectations for us. I believe in helping people understand the values of living a life that represents strong morals, and we can do that by being an example and not appearing like we are misrepresenting God's character traits. Personally, I just never want to offend people. We all have history and some people's life is a platform while others are not seen. I have found that some leaders who are called to serve God's people can tend to manipulate His Word for their benefit and that is not a good thing to do. I am not bashing leaders because I understand their calling and not all Pastors function that way, however, it is important for me to speak on this for the sake of awareness.

Salvation causes us to become grounded in our creator and teaches us the principles of living right. I have been blessed to have strong leader in my life and I am grateful for their teaching me to value my spiritual walk in a manner that is pleasing to God. I'm not saying you should not respect your pastor or serve your local church, but you must know that you are just as important to God as they are. You must study and learn God's Word for yourself. I discovered that my walk and salvation is personal, and I do not need to always get direction from a man or expose my issues. I had to learn how to be strong and wait on the voice of God. Sometimes the counsel of others can get you off track because they do not understand why you are doing things differently. I had to learn how to function in dysfunction whether it was in my personal or spiritual life and trust God to lead me out.

I have never really felt lost nor hopeless in my life, but I did feel empty after I had my son. I just did not have a solid plan for him or myself. I woke up every day with a desire to do my best and treat others with respect. I have always been that type of person. I never liked trouble nor wanted to be around it. I always wanted to do things the right way, but I did not have a clue what I was going to do with myself or my son. I didn't know how to raise him or provide for him. One day at my mother's house, I looked at my son and knew it was time for me to move out and raise him myself. It was important for me not to allow my mother to raise my son. He was fully my responsibility and my motivation, determination, dedication, and my reason for being the best mother I could be for him. Have you ever had a goal or task that inspired you so much that you wanted to make sure you did everything possible to make sure it would turn out right? Well, my son was my goal. I continued to work hard and make enough money until I found a place for my son and I to live in our own place. Things were going well at work and home, but something was still missing for me. I had a friend whose mother was a minister and when I visited them, her mother would always pull me to the side and talk about God. She saw something in me that I had not yet identified about myself. She told me that I was special, and God loved me. At the time, I had no idea what she was talking about. All I knew of God was to celebrate Him at Easter and Christmas. I had no idea that He loved me. I was not taught about Him in a personal way, however I was told about Him and His story was not even imaginable. All I heard was how bad I am and how good God is, and I should be grateful and never question anything about Him. I was never taught that I was a human and I was going to make mistakes, but God wanted me to try my best to live according to His word and not feel pressured. At that time most pastors would just tell me I needed to "receive what was being said and do it." Well, that was easier said than done. But my friend's mother made me feel connected with God when she shared His Love for me. I felt something in me wanting to learn more about what she was saying.

She invited me to share the Word of God with her one day a week.

The first scripture that I ever learned was John 3:16, "For God so loved the world that He gave His only begotten son that who so ever believes in Him shall be saved and have everlasting life." I had no idea what it meant but it was powerful like a surge of energy that went through my body. I was never the same. Did I know what that meant? NO, but I just knew it was something I wanted to do. I finally had an encounter with the love of God. At that point I knew the Creator had planted the "do right" spirit in me. I could not believe it. I was entering a place of understanding of who I was and why I was created. My desire to live a sweet, giving, and considerate life came from God. I started attending a church that was focused on teaching me how to live a holy lifestyle. I was so happy to go to church every week to hear about God and His goodness. I realized that I finally found something to be proud of instead of feeling ashamed. My salvation gave me confidence and I started talking about church and wanting to continue to learn more about God, His son, and the Holy Spirit. The funny thing is I had another friend whose mother was very spiritual as well and she also con-firmed what I didn't know about myself and that was the God in me. For the first time in my life I was eager to find out more about God and His purpose for me and my son. I was happy to know I wasn't alone or abandoned and I didn't have to be afraid anymore, because I knew God was with me. I am mirthful to share what salvation means to me because without it I would not have known how to raise my son, nor would I have become a responsible independent young adult. I had to find my own way of life and trust in a being that I could not see through faith. In this world you are expected to figure out who you are, what you want, where you are going to live, and how you are expected to take care of yourself. You get told what to do, but not how to do it. I had to figure out a lot of how to live on my own. Being a parent does not come with a manual. Salvation does not have any magical powers to take away the issues of life. Things were extremely overwhelming for me, but when I learned the love of God and His love toward me I knew I found my answer. Going to church and bible study became the norm for me and it caused me to keep drawing closer with the Holy Spirit living in me.

I must share the encounter that caused me to become a spirit-led woman of God. I attended the same church as my auntie. One Sunday morning we were at church and our pastor was not there on this particular day. There was an invitation to go to the altar if you wanted prayer. So, something came over me and I got up from my seat and felt myself going toward the front of the church. I was crying and everything. I was thinking to myself, God does not want me. I had a child and was not married and I was not good enough for His presence. I was full of shame, fear, and peace all at the same time. When I finally got to the front of the church there was a lady who asked me what I needed to pray for. I had no idea what I needed, all I knew was I felt drawn to go up for prayer. I was a 19-year-old with a small child no knowledge of what I was experiencing. At first, I was silent and then eventually said, "I want to give my life to God." I could not believe what I was saying nor how it looked. I just knew for the first time I was making the right decision for me and my son. Suddenly, this woman started praying for me and I had a feeling that I cannot explain to this day. Tears started streaming down my face and I felt something like heat going through my body. I felt like a feather - no weight, no worries, no fears. For the first time in my life I felt good about myself and I felt protected. I felt God. I felt loved. I felt hope. At that moment I was a new Lisa! I was in a new place and it felt good. The lady continued to pray for me and the last thing I remembered was speaking words that I did not know and ending up on the floor.

Now I understand that God had filled me with the Holy Spirit and gave me the power to speak in an unknown language. When I came to my natural self again I remember hearing a voice telling me, "It is well." My salvation is the meat of my life. It gives me the nutrients to be strong, determined, faithful, and committed with strength to endure (Ephesians 6:10). Connecting with the Creator I truly feel safe and protected. I am willing to let Him guide me, teach me, and discipline me because He knows what is best for me. I have learned how to trust, how to be willing, and how to obey God for my life. When we understand who we are and learn to walk in the identity that our Creator gave us, then our self-esteem will be strengthened. One way I learned how to stay committed with my salvation was when I studied the meaning of truth. We all must get up every day and get dressed before going out into the world. If not, we may deal with a lot of situations that we could have possibly avoided.

We protect our body by covering it with garments. When we commit to God, that is exactly what we need to do to our spiritual man. We must wake up early in the morning and clothe ourselves with the Word of God. I love Ephesians 6:10-18, it taught me how to prepare myself for the world. The first part to cover is the tongue. We must train our mouth to speak the truth and have a tone that will be received by others without causing them to be defensive. So, I had to tighten the belt (around my mouth) with truthfulness when I shared things with others. Lying only keeps a person in a pattern of deception. The word tells us to "Be strong in the Lord, and in the strength of his might." We cannot ever see clearly if we do not remember where our strength comes from. We must know that there is no power without HIM. God always has a strategic plan for us if we follow Him. In verse 11 it reads, "Put on the full armor of God, that ye may be able to stand against the wiles of the devil."

Now that we have power, God is trying to tell us how to prepare for the enemy and not lose focus, which means the enemy is full of illusions and tricks. Have you ever seen a magician do tricks and based on what you saw, it seemed like he was really causing stuff to disappear? That is like the enemy, he shows us things that appear real, and we believe them. The key is our belief. If we did not believe him then we would really see his tricks and then we would remember the power, we must rebuke his plans and get back on track. That leads me to the next part of this scripture. Verse 12 helps us to realize that our enemy is not people, it is evil powers, intentions, and forces used through others against us.

I really had to mature in this because I was always focused on how people treated me versus how their energy was. Once I became aware of how the enemy operated, I did not hold grudges with people. My focus was more on knowing that the enemy was trying to attack me. I had to be smarter than to think it was a person. We are just a vessel being used and because we are visual beings, it is easier to think it is a person coming against us instead of a spirit. Verse 13-14 tells us to put on spiritual armor because we must stand up against the enemy's plan.

God has a plan for us and it is a good one; the enemy has a plan as well and it is good for him. When we operate in wrongness we are the ones punished for it. I had to start asking myself questions like, "Why am I so willing to show the world a bad side of me instead of the good side?" When I did wrong things, I knew I did not anything to back me up. The enemy whispers in our spirits and then disappears once we act on it. Most of the time we do not look to the enemy for the bad things. Most of the time we say things like, "Why did God allow this bad thing to happen?" We lose complete thought of the enemy and channel everything to God. I had to learn that I have the power to make a good or bad choice. It is up to me on how I want to present myself. We must be positioned to walk in truth no matter what!

I am a Dr. Seuss fan because of his ability to educate young people with his books and quotes. Even as an adult I found myself still enjoying his quotes. There is one that reminds me to be truthful with myself and then I will be truthful with others. It is "Today you are you, that is truer than true. There is no one alive who is youer than you." We must be true to who we are and who we serve. If not, we will be programmed to believe in a lie about ourselves.

Ephesians 6:15 tells us to walk in peace. If we do this, we will not be disturbed when a shift happens. Having peace is agreeing with yourself and your creator. It is being on one accord in a situation. I had to adjust my thinking when my marriage ended because I was not at peace. I was always disturbed about something. I had to self-evaluate and deprogram my thinking. I knew I wanted to have a peaceful mindset and only God could give it to me. Verse 16 tells us we need to have a shield of faith so that we can stop all the plans of the wicked one. "Faith is the substance of things hoped for, and the evidence of things not seen." This is what we call our sixth sense. As humans we function by using our five natural senses, however, when we begin to walk in the spirit we need faith to help us fight off the enemy. When we execute our faith, it creates a stronger relationship with God because we must rely on Him to help us as we are facing trials and tribulations. Verse 17 focuses on salvation. The definition of salvation is the act of saving or protecting from harm, risk, loss, and destruction. Salvation is the connecting point of our relationship with Christ Jesus. It is a way for spirit-led people to exit from their old ways and choices and enter a more holistic way of living. Salvation reminded me that when I made bad choices, it was the mercy of my creator who forgave me and picked me back up. In our humanity, His grace and mercy are shown through our receiving His salvation.

I remember listening to a well-known spiritual speaker who told a story about a visit she had with a friend. She shared how a friend had invited them to come to town and forgot to mention that there was a train track near their hotel. The reason why the lady forgot to mention the train was because she lived near the track and was accustomed to the noise. It is important not to become desensitized to the voice of God. When we receive salvation, we must learn His voice. It is often like a still, small voice coming from within ourselves. We must read the bible as our guide to learning God's personality and characteristics. He is so unique with how He displays His ways to us. Being saved does not mean we have to live in a box, it teaches us how to function outside of the box. We learn a better way of living and we are truly led by our spirit versus our emotions. I have learned just how important it is to obey God and follow His purpose for our life. Serving God does not mean I am perfect, but it does mean He is and that I just need to be willing to live a "do right lifestyle" and obey Him by denying myself sometimes. As adults we are taught that we do not have to submit to anyone, because no one can tell us what to do. That is true to a certain degree. For example, I came to a point in my life where I did not have to listen to my parents' opinion about my life choices anymore, however, I forget that I still need guidance. I had to realize that my direction had to come from God and not my earthly parents anymore. Even though I was grown I still needed consistency in my life, and that caused me to have a more stable lifestyle. His words teach us how to be consistent. I had to trust God and learn to be patient with His plans for me. If you have not done so, surrender your thoughts, life, and actions over to the Creator and let Him direct your path. Do not put this off until tomorrow, do it today. Building a relationship with God is the best relationship you can ever have. People will come and go for whatever the reason, but God will stand with us and carry us through every moment we experience on this earth. In this world we will have trouble because of the fallen nature of man, but let God handle the impossible and trust Him with all your heart. The only way I am surviving is because I am fearless of men, and I am patient with God's will. I am watchful of the issues of life, and I am silent when God is giving me instructions. I must listen intently and if I talk too much I will not pay close attention to the directions. I have learned with God that I am not in control of my life. I am instructed to follow the guidelines in the bible and live up to them. As people we do have to take initiative to do things for ourselves and need to seek Him so that we will not be disappointed if things do not work out.

I remember when I was transitioning from working in the corporate world into the educational world. I had to pray about what I wanted to do and wait for an answer in my spirit. I knew I could apply for a teaching position, but the question was, "Am I ready for a new career path?" I knew my purpose was to serve, seek, and worship God. I also knew I had to do some things for myself and He would help me see it through. I knew once I got my answer from Him, He would do the rest. All He wants is for you to try this formula: FAITH + TRUST= SALVATION. It has helped me understand that suffering is a part of learning. Once I started paying attention to my life, things just started becoming clearer for me. I started eating good fruit. The Word says, "the fruit of the spirit is: love, joy, peace, patience, kindness, long-suffering, self-control, faithfulness and gentleness (Galatians 5:22-23). Against such there is no other law." I examined these attributes that I needed as a person who loves and serves God. These principles are very different from our human nature, because they are given to us by a spiritual being.

I had to learn how to become this person in my spirit-led lifestyle. It is hard to love someone who has hurt you, but once I learned what loves means to God, I understood why it was a struggle for me. I was depending on a human type of love which leads to a more intimate physical attraction. Then I learned about God's way of love which is showing kindness. This type of love reflects having a good will and de-votion to others. My intentions concerning love were wrong and that is why it was hard for me to love those who hurt me. God's type of love freed me to show care to others whether they deserved it or not. Once I started operating in love then God dealt with me about what joy is. He told me I cannot be strong without His joy because it is not like being happy. It is deeper than that, because joy really is gladness and is not determined by what is good or bad in life. I had to focus on God's purpose for me and not my situation. Having joy meant when things are bad I could still smile about it.

The next fruit that was hard but necessary to eat was peace. I had to understand that it did not remove problems from happening, it simply gave me an imperturbability that was unexplainable. It took me to a place of wholeness and serenity. I knew that God was handling all the events in my life for that day. I had to stop feeling so frazzled over the turbulence that was going on in my life. I had to allow Him to speak to my spirit. In this 21st century world everything is quick and fast. We can go out to eat and want to be served instantly. We have no time to wait because we have become accustomed to the get-it-quick mentality. When we commit our spirit to the fruit of God we must learn how to have patience. I found that when I did not accept forbearing situations, I could not handle things that well. I would become easily frustrated and everything caused me to get upset. Patience is a part of longsuffering because it helped me to stop lashing out and to stop sweating the small stuff and pray more. If I was not patient, I found myself being unkind to others. God's way is kindness and He wants all of us to eat this fruit on a daily basis. If we do this, our world would not be so unkind. I really love being kind to people and seeing them change from looking mean to smiling and saying, "have a good day." I found that when I compliment people who look unkind, they end up smiling and speaking to me. Showing kindness turns off the energy of being negative. It will diffuse any ugly intentions.

Another fruit that is good for your spirit but could be hard to do is faithfulness. It is really an act of loyalty and commitment. It shows if a person has integrity or not. It is not hard for me to be faithful because that is my nature, and it was so hard for me to accept that everyone else could not operate that way. If a person commits themselves to God, He will help you become faithful. Only God can give you faithfulness, because it belongs to Him.

Gentleness is another fruit of the spirit. I remember my dad telling my siblings and I that "meekness is not a weakness." Being gentle is not a gender role either. Some people think if you are soft spoken you are not a strong person. However, gentleness can cause a person to be at peace even when others are not. That leads me to the last fruit which is self-control. I tell my children and students to not be so concerned about others that you forget about yourself. For example, children love to come and tell what others are doing, so I help them to get on the right track by asking them, "Does this matter concern you?" If they answer "no", then I tell them to only be concerned with themselves. I say this because we cannot control others, however, we can control ourselves. That is why I love the serenity prayer. It says "God Grant me the serenity to accept the things I cannot change (which are others), the courage to change the things I can (which is yourself), and the wisdom to know the difference. It is important to have self-control and pull away from a situation that could cause more harm than good. I have been living this spirit-led lifestyle for over 27 years and I cannot complain one bit! I know without God I am nothing. I have a prayer life and before requesting His guidance I always remember to enter His gates with thanksgiving and His courts with praise! I want to live in the spirit. I don't want to fight what is right for me. I want to walk in the fruit of the spirit, because it causes me to accept things and not judge them. The fruit of the spirit can only be eaten when we surrender to the Creator, because it belongs to Him. So, if you are trying to do it yourself and you feel like you are not achieving these attributes, it is because you cannot do it without Him. "There is nothing as comforting in life nor as sweet, loving, giving, touching, or peaceful as calling on the name of Jesus in Prayer!" LWB Beckwith

MASTERMIND

1. What are some things that you do to help people the way God intended you to? Explain.

2. Are you a person who only receives and never gives? Explain

3. What does salvation mean to you?

4. Do you have to be happy or have joy in your life? Explain.

5. Does everything have to go smoothly in your life before you have joy? Explain

6. How do you handle problems in your life? Explain.

7. How do you show kindness to others? Explain.

8. Do you always have to be in charge? Explain.

9. How important is your level of protein (salvation) and does it help you to keep reaching higher?

FINISH THESE SENTENCES:

1.   I am determined to walk in the spirit because

   _______________________________________.

2.   Salvation means _______________________

   _______________________________________.

3.   I will only control myself because ________

   _______________________________________.

SCRIPTURES U – W:

U – Unto Thee, O God, do we give thanks. – Psalm 75:1

V – Verily, verily, I say unto you, Whatsoever ye shall ask the Father in My name, He will give it you. – John 16:23

W – What time I am afraid, I will trust in Thee. – Psalm 56:3

CHAPTER SEVEN

DESSERT COURSE

"It is time to Live and not Exist!"

L.I.F.E.

Lasting Impressions Forever Enjoyed

This dish is served after a meal. It is a confectionary taste that creates a burst of energy and even a feeling of happiness due to the increased release of serotonin which happens after we consume carbohydrates. The dessert phase of life encourages people to live in the moment and experience happy events by becoming more conscious of their surroundings while not focusing on negative emotions like anxiety. "God formed the man from the dust of the ground and breathed into his nostrils the breath of life and the man became a living being." (Genesis 2:7) This is the first sign of life for each of us every morning. Most of us are satisfied with just waking up and taking a deep breath (existing). Reading that scripture helped me understand that living simply means we were designed to exist, but if we want to experience adventurous things we need to take risks. There are things that can hinder us from living such as doubt, fear, and lack of care for oneself. We should be joyful every day of life not because we woke up, but instead because of the creativity that is in us to explore what we woke up to.

I found out that it is important not to let others limit you. It is good to fulfill your dreams and go after them by chasing what you want without being afraid. I remember having a conversation with someone who made me feel like what I was doing was not good enough and I needed to make sure that God was okay with it. It really confused me because I try to make decisions that are pleasing to God. I had to deal with the possibility that what I wanted may not be congenial to God. One day He spoke to my spirit and told me that He created me to explore what I liked and that it was okay for me to live and be adventurous. God told me that if I was not harming myself and others, then no problem existed. So, if I wanted to change some things around in my life, that was fine, and all I had to do was be at peace with it. At that point, I was delivered from others' thoughts about what was best for me. I learned that just because someone suggested something, does not mean I have to comply. It showed me that what I was doing was good enough for God and me. In His word He said, "I will instruct thee and teach thee in the way which thou shalt go: I will counsel thee with mine eyes upon thee." After reading that, I was set free from others' thoughts on what I should and should not do for my life. I had to learn to seek counseling from my spirit. I noticed that many of my decisions were really based on others. I had to become confident and calm down so that my spirit would work for me instead of my emotions and others' ideas. My spirit is my first instinct, therefore I had to make sure that I was aware of how I would listen to my emotions. When I stopped doubting spirit, I became more adventurous. Life is a big test and it is up to you to either pass or do a retake. If you fail and fall, it is ok, all you must do is get up and try it again. Think of a baby who is trying to walk. They fall more than they walk in the beginning, but once they keep practicing it becomes easier for them. One day they start walking more and falling less. That is what living is all about. We will make some decisions that are not always the best for us, and that is okay because there is always something to learn from. Mistakes can make us feel uncertain about something and cause us to derail by questioning ourselves, but just remember we are human, and we will mess up sometimes. I had to be confident in my Creator when that happens, because if not I would fall into a deeper hole that could be harder to get out of. I had to learn to live my life, because I knew what was inside of me and what I wanted to try. We have all been shopping at some point in our lives and before we purchase the product we may try it on to make sure it fits and that we are comfortable in it. That is the same with our decisions, we must try things to see if we really like it or not. If it is not good for us, most of the time we leave it alone. Otherwise we will become oblivious to it and just deal with it until we explode. Life is not intended to be a cannon bomb, so try not to put so much pressure on yourself and cause a reaction that you know will not be good for you. When others try to give you their advice on what they think you should do, you can kindly say that you will take that into consideration. If you like what you hear, then good, if not, oh well. It is truly your call. I had to stop being in bondage and learn to live my life like others were living theirs. I had to learn how to "Live life with the mindset of stretching yourself as long as your neck will take you!" LWB Butterfly. Taking a risk is not a bad thing nor is it disappointing to God. He created us to be free to live.

Another area that stops us from living is fear. I had to learn how not to allow a person to dictate my life nor allow manipulation to trick me into missing new things. When I started my undergrad program, I had a very dear person tell me that I should not do it because I had small children and they needed me. Well, If I would have followed their thoughts about my actions, I would never have earned my degree. I could not be intimidated by their thoughts nor let them interfere with my life choices. It was a good feeling to decide what was best for my life and not just exist and do what that person thought was best for me.

It was not always that easy for me to decide to do what was best for me. I had to get counseling at one point because I felt like I was all over the place. I felt like fear was overtaking me and I had to slow things down. So, I went to get some support from a therapist and that helped me to level myself out. There were techniques that I had to do such as: taking deep breaths in and out and counting to ten before I could speak. That practice really helped me calm down and gather my thoughts. I realized that what I was allowing myself to do was to panic over things that were a simple fix by taking a deep breath, gathering my thoughts, and sharing what I wanted. I was learning how to detox my way of thinking and lifestyle. The deep breaths were helping me exchange negativity for peace. I was tired of existing in fear of not doing things right, and overthinking everything to the point that I did nothing. I had to make some serious changes about what life meant to me and if I was going to either keep existing or learn how to live.

I remember my mom having a routine for everything that we did, and if she did not follow it I thought something was wrong. Let me share a funny, but not so funny story with you about how my family and I functioned when I was growing up. We had a family member stay with us for a while and she brought something to our attention one day. She shared with us our routine that we followed verbatim every day. When I got home from work, I came in the house, took off my work clothes, showered, ate, watched T.V., then went to bed. She told me that my mom, sister, and I did the exact same thing every day. It was funny how we all had adopted the same conventional way of existing every evening. What was so hilarious was that we did not even know we were doing that. We just got so accustomed to doing what was the norm for us. When I moved out, I found myself doing that with my family as well. I was living my life in autopilot mode. I would do the same thing day after day. I even traveled the same way to work and would get mad if I had to do anything differently. Typically, that type of lifestyle showed that a person was consistent and stable. It was very comfortable for me until my children started getting older and I needed to do activities with them. I became afraid to do things differently. I did not want to be flexible because I thought that meant I was not being a stable parent. Fear once again was settling in my spirit, simply because I was unfamiliar with how to adjust my life's schedule. I did not know how to do that because I had never seen it done. Everything would change, and I did not know how to handle that. I remember one time when I was married, my husband wanted to buy us a washing machine and dryer and I literally got upset with him. I guess you are thinking, why would she get upset over getting that. Well, I was used to going to the laundry mat and when he said we were not doing that anymore, it really caused me to feel nervous. I had to do some soul searching and I later found out that it was because I was being introduced to something that I had never done before. I could do laundry right in my home and that felt great. I began to think about what other things I was afraid to try. I had to learn how to break myself free from me. I was willing to stop living in a box and see how things could be done differently, and it worked out for my good. After that experience I learned how to be open minded and willing to explore things. One thing I had to start doing was take care of myself and do things for me. Another thing the therapist helped me realize was that I needed some me time. I love working out and I decided to take at least 30 minutes a day and spend time with myself. I have learned that, "Being alone is not a taboo, it is really more about getting to know you." LWB Butterfly. I was never really an outdoor kind of person, but I learned how to appreciate nature. I would go on trails and walk for hours. Nature is beautiful to see and hear. It shows just how powerful God really is and how to enjoy what He gave us. The scenery is so beautiful, peaceful, and caused me to appreciate His work of art. It was important for me to understand what living looks like, because I was tired of just existing. Life is filled with exploring and using wisdom by being free and cautious at the same time. As a parent I was always cautious of every move that my children made, and it was important for me to allow them to be free as well. I know at times they did not like how I was always concerned about everything that they did. I did that because I was nervous (fearful) about what might go wrong and I wanted to protect them. I realize that my fears were causing me not to show my children how to live a free and fun life. I did not show them that taking risks and being spontaneous was okay. I had to show myself and my children that some things in life we must come outside of our comfort zone to do. I was learning how to take a chance and live my life a little differently than how I was raised.

One thing I remember taking a risk on was switching from a job to a career, because I knew it was going to be a major financial cut and I was nervous about doing it. I had to decide and said I was either going to be happy doing what I love and find a way to restore the wages lost or I was going to stay where I was and just exist in the job I was in. I jumped in the deep end and surprised myself. Not only did I not have financial struggles, I became an owner of a tutoring and summer enrichment program. If I would not have taken that risk and lived out my passion, I would still be at the job today and not the owner of a company nor an author of a book. I was tired of existing.

Life is such a mystery and trying to live it without guidance may be risky, but it is okay. You will find out just like I did that it is worth the adventure. It causes you to do things that you did not even know were possible. I am now fulfilling a dream that I never thought could be a reality. If you are chasing your dream, do not give up on you. It will come at the right time, and in the meantime just keep living it out on your drawing board, in your mind, and just know that one day it will manifest. While you are waiting try not to allow boredom to settle in. Volunteer in the area that you are trying to pursue to keep your fire lit. One day my friend suggested that I should try things before I say how I feel about them. That made so much sense. How could I possibly not like something that I had never tried? I am not afraid to have an open mind by trying new things. There are times when you must take chances and step out to see if you will sink or stand. When I changed careers, I was clueless as to how I was going to be an educator, however, what I did know about myself was that I am a trainable, intelligent, willing, organized, loving, and patient person who was ready to enrich children's lives. All I needed was a strong educational background to help enhance my capabilities. "When you know who you are, your confidence will cause you to not be afraid to try something new!" LWB Butterfly What I know about myself gave me confidence to try the unknown. When I first went into the classroom being a lead teacher I was unsure of many things, but one thing I was sure of was that I was going to do my best and if I needed support I was going to ask. It was okay for me to have gone into my classroom for the first time and be nervous about what I was going to teach and how I was going to teach it. That is a normal reaction, because I had never done it before. Once I started getting trained, I began to develop in the areas that I was struggling in. As a teacher, I share with my students that the purpose of you being in my class is not that you already know everything, instead it is for you to learn, and it is okay to not know something. I tell them that it is a part of their educational growth. I was intimidated by my teachers, and I said that I will not make my students feel like that. It took me several years before I earned my degree in education and it was worth the wait. Life is about living in the moments that we experience, not in the timing of them. I was in my mid 30's and that did not stop me from becoming an educator. I took a risk and it came at the right time in my life. My degree was delayed, but it was not denied. I would never have thought that I could graduate with honors nor be working toward my masters now. I had to hold myself accountable live by this: "Make a decision today and do not complain about the outcome. It is what YOU wanted." LWB Butterfly   I am so glad that I was willing to try. If I did not just stop and enjoy the things around me, I probably would still be wishing and saying, "what if." I am living a very fulfilled life now. Even writing this book is fulfilling, whether it becomes a #1 seller or not. What matters to me is that I became an author and was able to share my story. I had to create myself a seven-step reminder to follow as I was achieving my life goals. I had to prepare and care for myself and stop being afraid. I had to come to terms with some things inwardly that were reflected outwardly. In life we must be courageous. "A roaring lion is like life. It makes you fear the sounds and yet gives you courage to confront the situation" LWB Butterfly. I know that some things in my life were created because of some of the energy that I was dealing with.

First, I had to remove all types of negative thought patterns that were forming, because it caused me to feel entrapped by them. Therefore, I could not see myself growing and going in the direction that I want on my new journey. Next, I had to make sure I was taking care of myself financially and being wise with how I spent my money. A lot of times we cannot live an adventurous life because we do not have money to do things. Saving is not a bad thing to do. I remember having to make a major decision about my house and it was because I was not financially stable enough to make the necessary adjustments I needed to because I did not have money in place to cover the cost. I know a lot of people who have ended relationships because of financial promises that were broken. For me to feel like I was living, I had to make sure I had a concrete plan for my life. I did not want to live a life full of regret. When I went back to school, I had to make sure my children were okay and that I did not have to deal with any unnecessary interruptions that would cause me to be delayed with graduating. I was pacing myself strategically because I wanted to make sure that my plans were going to be very successful. Then, I felt ready and prepared to begin my new way of living. I was ready to walk toward my new path. As I said before, I did not realize that my career was really going to cause me to become an owner of an educational program. Before any of that could happen, I had to make sure I was positioned correctly so that I could avoid any unresolved issues. I was well prepared for my possibilities and could not be afraid anymore. God told me that He did not give me a spirit of fear, so that meant if I had any it was coming out based upon my lack of trust in His abilities for me. I could not fool myself anymore nor lie to myself because I was afraid to say I was afraid to take risks.

Fear is a negative emotion that causes us to do nothing. I identified that I was not scared to live an adventurous life. I know most of us think adventure means jumping out of an airplane or climbing a mountain or any other type of over-the-top activity. But, it really is just having enough courage to do what you think is the impossible. I remember when God spoke to me about running my own summer program. I was walking with a dear friend of mine and I told her that the summer was coming, and I needed to make sure my family was going to be okay for the season. I had to find a summer job at a school. At that time, I was not used to being off work, let alone not having any income. Then suddenly God spoke to my spirit and told me not to look for a school, but for me to create my own. I followed His voice and it was extremely hard the first three years, but then doors started opening and I went well past the numbers that I had set for myself. It is so good to hear the voice of God and obey it. I am sharing this with you because we all need to be encouraged. There may be someone right now who is afraid of stepping out on faith and doing what they think is impossible. I am here to say go for it. God will pro-vide and set you up with the best team possible. I know I am the author of this book, but God has placed phenomenal people in my life and I am forever grateful for them. Each person poured into my dream and it was not about their success, instead they showed me they wanted to be part of what God had for me. They showed me love and for that I want to make sure I do the same for others. Love can be represented in many ways, but for me, this quote rings loudly: "Letting Others Vibe Eagerly is showing the act of (L.O.V.E.)." LWB Butterfly

People express their care through their own energy. Seeing how people offered to support me showed how much they valued me and what I was to do. That is why I want to be as transparent and not appear like life has not caused me some ups and downs, twists and turns, ins and outs. I just want to help lead the way toward your newness. Now if you are ready for your change from existing to living I know the sky is your limit and it is untouchable, yet achievable. My son shared with me one time that he wanted someone to help him with what he was going through, and I told him that others can help you, but he must challenge himself first. He had to learn to be the first person to care about himself. He could not just be relying on me or others to say something to help build him up. He had to look in the mirror and do it for himself. We all must learn how to encourage ourselves. I hope that you reflect on this list I gave you and learn how to show up in your own life and celebrate all that you are doing. The main voice of reasoning we should hear about our life choices is God's. Remember, others are great resources in our lives, but when it comes to living it out, that part is up to us. We do not need unsolicited advice, especially if it is going to get us off track. Your decisions may make you feel uncomfortable at first like mine did, but the more you practice, the easier it becomes. I had to learn not to allow my emotional state of comfort to cause me not to try new things. We only have one life and we must live each stage out, even if we do not want to. What I have found is that it is easier to identify who I am and who I belong to. Do not allow yourself to just exist by waking up, and merely breathing and doing the same daily chores. Take control of yourself, have fun, and do something different every so often. I had to stop fearing and existing and start living and I am living my life in such a healthier way now. So can you. It is time to live and eat this dessert called life and enjoy every single mouthful. "Life is to serve and be served" LWB Butterfly.

MASTERMIND

1.   How do you feel after eating your dessert (moments of life)?

2.   How can you live in greatness?

3.   How is living and existing different for you?

4.   When is a time you felt adventurous?

FINISH THESE SENTENCES:

1.   When I start to live I will______________

_________________________________.

2.   When I do______________ I feel like I am living.

3.   I will not stop myself from ____________
____.

4.   Fun to me is ______________________.

SCRIPTURES X – Z:

X – Exceeding great and precious promises are given unto us. – 2 Peter 1:4

Y – Ye are the light of the world – Matthew 5:14

Z – Zion heard, and was glad. – Psalm 97:8

ABOUT THE AUTHOR

Lisa W. Beckwith is an Author, Educator, CEO, Certified Life Coach, and Founder of the Transcendent Enrichment and Tutoring Program. Lisa provides heart-felt encouragement and wise counsel when speaking with others about their life choices. Her first book, *Food For L.I.F.E (Lasting Impressions Forever Enjoyed)* was released in 2018.

Lisa is a devoted mother of four wonderful gifts from God. Her children are strong individuals with great character traits, talents and creativities. For booking and more information about Lisa, please visit www.lisabeckwith.com.

I am come that they might have L.I.F.E. and that they might have it more abundantly. (John 10:10)
It's your time now.

www.ingramcontent.com/pod-product-compliance
Lightning Source LLC
Chambersburg PA
CBHW061504050726

47593CB00002B/448